THE BOYS OF THE BONE YARD SLASH

THE EAST TEXAS CONNECTION

featuring

BUBBA, JASON & OTHER CHARACTERS

by

Ronald Armstrong

Dorrance Publishing Co
585 Alpha Drive
Suite 103
Pittsburgh, PA 15238
Visit our website at *www.dorrancebookstore.com*

ISBN: 978-1-6393-7431-1
eISBN: 978-1-6393-7492-2

This book is dedicated to my Brothers
who are gone but not forgotten.

"Red" Ainsworth
Dennis Stewart
Daryl "Pee Wee" Peery

PREFACE

As of right now, October 19, 2019, I have lived half of my life close to the Bone Yard Slash located on the Red River in the Chicota, Texas, and I've lived the latter half of my life in East Texas. Tyler and Hawkins is where I call home nowadays. I have been blessed to have met and befriended and been befriended by as many colorful characters here as I did where I grew up! I have a ton of stories about these East Texas folks whom I love and who are as big a part of me as my friends and family from the Bone Yard Slash!

East Texas is full of big Pine trees, oil fields, gas wells, rivers, swamps, hardwood hollers and great people! Lots of good ole' boys and girls! Some of these folks have become my family and I wouldn't trade them for diamonds or gold! Once again, some names have been changed, a few places have been changed....BUT (yes, there's a "but" again!) this story is all true... these things really happened!

If you find yourself or someone you know in my book and the name or place is different—-then, that's *your* secret!

ALL MEN HAVE ONE THING IN COMMON...

THEY ERR!!

BUBBA

YES! A story about someone in East, Texas named "Bubba"—-imagine that!

I could write a book about my buddy Bubba, but right now we will stick with just a few stories. He won't be given a first name as he is so very famous in East Texas; everyone knows him. I will call him "Curious Bubba" like the monkey "Curious George".

BUBBA & THE SHARK TANK

My buddy, Bubba and I have spent a lot of time together—-even the bad times were good times with Bubba. Bubba aka Luscious Hard Body; Struggle Bubba; Bubba Licious; Curious Bubba had an array of other names he gave himself or was pinned on him by other people.

We took a short trip to Galveston with my wife, two daughters, Bubba and his wife and two daughters, along with about ten other girls who ranged in age from nine to twelve years of age. We were having a great time at the aquarium and all the children were being well-behaved—-except Bubba of course! We were looking at the sharks which were in an enclosed glass water tank with a rope barrier surrounding it. The tank was about six feet in height with an open top. Bubba was not satisfied with the view as all the sharks were staying in the back of the tank and would occasionally glide by for an "up close" look. Bubba climbed over the rope barricade and up one side of the shark tank. He then began to splash the water with his hand while holding onto the tank with his other hand!

"What are you doing, Bubba?" I asked.

"I want a better look at those sharks. I'm trying to get them over here closer." he replied.

About this time a security guard comes running over and parts the children like Moses and the Red Sea. He began shouting, "Sir! Sir! Get down from there and stop splashing the water!"

Bubba continues splashing the water and tries to reason with the guard, explaining that he only wants a better look at the sharks. The guard is not impressed and shouts, "Sir, if you don't get down and move to the outside of the barrier, I'm going to have to arrest you!"

"OK! Fine!, Bubba said.

As he climbed down and returned to the other side of the barrier, he was steadily complaining about not being able to see the sharks "up close". The guard returned to his station and all the children were standing there watching with amazement.

"OK kids, now you see how *not* to act at the aquarium." I told them. Bubba just smiled his usual mischievous smile and continued to joke and play with the kids. YES! Bubba needs a guardian at all times!

WALMART—-BUBBA—-MOONWALK

On one such trip as mentioned above (I think we were in Corpus Christi), one of the wives needed to stop at Walmart., Everyone remained in the van and waited on her—-except Bubba. Yes, Bubba decided he needed to show the children his dance moves. Since Bubba is almost always barefooted, he could move around freely and quickly (or so he thought). Bubba danced the Moonwalk, and he did it quite well,l I will have to admit. The children cheered and I clapped. This encouraged him to continue.

He Moonwalked down one side of the van, around the front and down the other side while we watched and cheered. I failed to mention that Bubba had partaken of several adult beverages, "Scubby Snacks" he affectionately calls them. After several minutes of Moonwalking on warm asphalt and a minor attempt at break dancing, the wife returned, and we were on our way. It was late in the day and the vacation activities and Bubba's antics had us worn out, so we turned in for a good night's sleep.

The next morning, we all got up and started wrangling kids and Bubba. Bubba come out of the bathroom, hair sticking up all over his head, no shirt, no shorts and barefooted. He is walking like he is on a frozen pond and the ice is cracking! Easing along at a snail's pace was highly unusual for Bubba as he is usually "off the walls".

"My feet are killing me! What did I do last night?" he asked.

Before we could answer, he showed us the bottoms of his feet, and we could see that all the hide was raked off of them!

"My feet are killing me!" he repeated. "I can hardly walk!" he said.

I was laughing so hard that I was crying. We told him about the great performance that he put on for us in the parking lot and how the mile of Moon Walking must have peeled the hide from his feet.

"Let's get to the beach and let the salt water heal your feet," I said.

"Y'all don't let me do that no more! Bubba said.

"Yeah! Right, like we can control Curious Bubba," I replied.

BUBBA & THE FIREPLACE

My buddy, Bubba, is a germaphobe; a clean freak; a neat nut and anything else that you can think of that describes someone who likes everything clean, neat and in order at all times. Bubba and family had moved in a new house with a fireplace. It was a very nice house, and I was very glad for him. The weather had begun to get cool enough for a fire, and I pulled up at Bubba's house to find three or four smoldering sticks of firewood lying outside the back door of his home. (I can hardly write this as I'm laughing already!). I look up and here comes Bubba around the house with a piece of I-beam steel that he has cut a hole in and tied on a long rope. (Yeah—-shit's fixin' to get funny—-hang on!). Anyway, I asked Bubba, "What's up with the firewood?"

"Well, I started a fire in the fireplace for the first time. I got it going real good, real fast", he said. "Then the house filled up with smoke! So, I was trying to get the wood out of the fireplace and throw it outside. But I couldn't get it with my hands. I threw water on it and that makes it worse. I run and get my welding gloves and manage to carry it outside without setting the house on fire or burning the light-colored carpet in the living room!" he said.

"OK, so what's with the I-beam and rope?" I asked.

"Well, I think the chimney's stopped up with a bird's nest. I'm going to climb up on the roof and throw this I-beam and rope down the chimney and clear it out," he said as he finished tying a knot in the rope.

"You sure that's the problem?" I asked.

"Gotta be," Bubba replied.

"OK, I hope it works," I replied as Bubba climbed up on the roof.

Bubba climbed up on the roof and made his way over to the chimney. He dropped the thirty-pound I-beam down the chimney, and we heard a loud, "CLANG"! Bubba fished the I-beam back up the chimney and proceeded to launch the "weapon of doom" down again, and again a loud metallic "CLANG" was heard. Every time it CLANGED Bubba would squint his eyes like a monkey and pop his head around and look at me.

After the second CLANG, I said, "Bubba, your damper is closed!" Bubba reeled in his I-beam fishing apparatus and said, "Dang! I think you're right!"

He scampered off the roof like Cheetah in a Tarzan movie, ran in the house and stuck his head in the fireplace with a flash light, then flipped the damper lever to clear the chimney.

BUBBA & ME—-ARRESTED ON THE PEASE RIVER

My buddy, Bubba, will get you in a tight spot every now and then…but he will also help you get out of a tight spot.

I love you, Bubba.

Yeah, anyone who knows Bubba, knows that there are very good odds that at some point you could get arrested if you run with him for very long periods of time.

Well, one November, Bubba and I and another fellow (I'll call him, Fred) decided to go out toward Paducah, Texas and go deer hunting. Around the Pease River, the whitetail and the mule deer overlap, and you can hunt both. So, with dreams of wall hanging bucks on our minds, we made plans. Bubba borrowed a Dodge four-door diesel pickup from a friend. Fred borrowed a 7mm magnum rifle from one of his friends. We loaded up other rifles, food, ammo, and sleeping bags and headed out. We drove all night and pulled into Dumas, Texas at daylight. We wanted to check out the panhandle before heading South toward Matador and Paducah.

The sun was coming up, it was thirty degrees, and the wind was blowing. Bubba had on insulated overalls, his hair was sticking up in all directions and he was barefooted…yes! barefooted. He got out at a convenience store and asked about where he could get breakfast. Fred and I stayed in the truck. We observed as the lady behind the counter was looking Bubba up and down, pausing to stare at his feet as she talked with him and continued to gaze with a look of disbelief while he made his exit.

Bubba scampered back out to the truck like a pet monkey and jumped in. He began to tell us where to find some breakfast. We headed that way, and I asked Bubba if he had a comb.

"Why do I need a comb?" he asked.

"Because you look like a damn, wild man, that's why," I told him.

Bubba began licking the palms of his hands and trying to slick down his wild ass looking rug. "How's that?" he asked.

I looked at Fred. Fred just shrugged. "That's fine, Bubba," I replied, even though it was still sticking up and covered with spit now.

"My feet are freezing!" Bubba complained.

"Put some freaking boots on!" Fred suggested.

"But my feet get hot when I'm riding," Bubba said. Fred and I just both shook our heads.

We ate, surveyed some grasslands in the panhandle and headed toward Matador. Mesquite trees, plains and small canyons were pleasant scenery as we headed toward Paducah.

Fred's Uncle had a little spread and a cattle operation outside Paducah in Cottle County. Fred's Uncle was friendly and hospitable. He complained that the mule deer were a problem along the highway and always causing accidents. "Y'all should just shoot your deer off the side of the road after dark," he suggested. "That's the easiest way to do it." Then he laughed, "Y'all can go down to the Pease River and hunt from cut bank to cut bank for one hundred miles."

Fred had hunted here before, so we set out to the Pease River. We parked under the bridge and decided to do some scouting upriver. We spread out and found lots of sign, deer tracks, hog tracks, turkey, bobcat, lots of game. We met back up at a certain spot and headed back to the truck. Bubba with his helter-skelter hairdo was looking through his binoculars. He looked toward the bridge where we were parked and said, "Hey! There's a Game Warden looking at us through his binoculars!"

"Well, quit looking at him, Bubba," I suggested.

So, what does Bubba do? He continues to watch the game warden and waves at him. No big deal…but not what I would do.

We get to the bridge and the Game Warden meets us. "Hi, where you boys from?" he asked.

"Texas!" Bubba replies before Fred and I have a chance to answer.

"No shit!" the Game Warden says,

"You'll have to excuse him," I interject and quickly explain to him that we are from Hawkins, just north of Tyler.

The Warden's pissed demeanor relaxed a little, and we introduced ourselves and showed our hunting licenses. Bubba had the super combo hunting license, which he pointed out to the Warden.

"I can read," the Warden said.

Bubba explained that he was a truck driver and that's why he said that he was from Texas. "I drive all over the U.S. and that's what people want to know…what state I'm from," he said.

The Warden was not impressed as Bubba had gotten off on the wrong foot. "You boys can hunt the East side of the bridge from cut bank to cut bank, but you can't hunt west of the bridge, the direction you came from," he explained.

"OK, sounds good, thank you," we replied and headed in the direction he had pointed us to.

The temperature dropped, and a light snow began to fall. We hunted until dark and met back at the truck. We decided to build a fire and camp under the bridge. We would get an early start in the morning and hopefully, see some mule deer or whitetails. I cooked up some dinner while Fred and Bubba had some adult beverages and then opened a bottle of peach brandy that Bubba and I had gotten down in Old Mexico (that's another story). We ate, drank and had a lotta laughs. The night was going good. Fred ran out of snuff and decided we needed to drive into Paducah. It was only about fifteen or twenty miles away. (Paducah ain't real big, folks).

On the way into town at about 11p.m., we saw two mule deer on the side of the road. One is a nice 4x5 buck. (Ya'll see where this is going right?) On this highway, you can see for miles...I mean actual miles! Ain't no traffic, nothing coming or going for miles in either direction. We spin around and Fred slides his 7mm out the window and WHOOM! The buck runs across the highway in front of us and Bubba takes a shot... WHOOM! and WHAP! He connects! The buck stumbles through the ditch and falls on the outside of the barbed wire fence. I run over to the buck and cut his throat to make sure he is dead. We were elated and dreaming of back strap and eggs in the morning. We leave the deer on the spot and head into town for snuff.

Now folks, whatever you want to think about me, I've killed a lot of deer out of season and past the limit during season. But me and my family ate every bite of it. That was a different time and place. I never got caught. Most of these were with a .22 caliber rifle.

On the way back to camp, we pick up the deer and go about our business. Yeah, we should have left it there and picked it up the next morning. We get back to camp, examine the deer again and throw some wood on the fire. We're standing around the fire talking and laughing. It's 12:30 a.m., below freezing, a light snow falling again. We see headlights heading our direction on the dirt road beside the highway that leads under the bridge. The truck stops with its headlights shining on us. Two Game Wardens get out and identify themselves as "Federal Game Wardens."

"How you boys doing?" they asked.

"We're fine," we replied.

Several minutes of small talk take place and eventually one of the wardens walks over to our truck and shines a light in the back. "Who's deer?" he asks.

By this time, Bubba had walked over to him and said, "You ain't goin' believe this, somebody gave us that deer."

Everything kinda' went into slow motion for me at this point. I looked at Fred. Fred looked at me. I said, "He didn't just say, 'You ain't gonna' believe this' did he?"

At that same instant, a Game Warden grabbed Bubba by the arm and spun him like a top, slammed him against the side of the truck and said, "You're under arrest!"

Bubba is trying to turn around and convince the Warden that it ain't our deer. (Yeah, it gets worse.)

"All y'all get over here and put your hands up where we can see them!", one of the Wardens ordered. We stood beside the truck as they took the deer's temperature, (yeah, it was way too high to have been shot before dark on a day below freezing with snow falling).

"Who shot the deer?" a warden inquired. No one was talking, except Bubba. He was still trying to convince them that someone had given us the deer. They told him that he need to "shut up", that he was making it worse. "You're all under arrest," they said.

They read us our rights and asked to see our driver's license and hunting license. Bubba, once again, pointed out that he had purchased the Super Combo Package Texas Hunting License. The Warden pointed out that it didn't make a damn, because it doesn't allow you to shoot deer at night! They examined our guns and smelled the barrels but couldn't determine which one had been the gun to fire the shot. So, they took all our guns and arrested all of us because none of us would admit to being the shooter. Remember folks, Fred's gun has been borrowed from a friend and the truck we're driving is borrowed. The Wardens load our guns up and take the deer, They drive away leaving us standing on the banks of the Pease River holding paperwork by a dying fire in the falling snow at one o' clock in the morning.

I looked at Fred and said, "They forgot us!" Fred looked at the disappearing taillights and then looked at me. "Yeah, they did!" he said.

They arrested us, but they didn't take us with them. I don't get it," I said.

Bubba was still complaining that they took his deer and that was the first mule deer he'd ever killed.

"I think that's the least of our problems!" Fred said.

We stood by the fire and looked at our paperwork with a flashlight, thinking that might clarify things or that they may turn around and come back to get us. We cussed and discussed the situation and after an hour we decided to go to sleep. Feeling like I had been gut punched, I found it hard to sleep, not to mention that Bubba snores like a freight train.

Morning came, and we gathered up our belongings to head home. With no licenses and no guns, there was no sense in staying for the remainder of our trip that we planned. We headed home knowing that our wives were going to be pissed and Fred would have to explain to his friend why he didn't bring his 7mm rifle back. The upside was that they didn't impound the borrowed truck we were driving, and they didn't take us to jail, even though they arrested us. (Come to find out the Cottle County jail is closed at night, and no one is on duty. They didn't want to wake Jim Bob up to open the jail, I guess.)

The Pease River Incident

(Part Two)

The story doesn't end that easily or that soon. Cottle County only has court every three months, not a lot going on in that part of the world, I guess.

We get notices that we need be in court in Cottle County on February 14th! Yes! Valentine's Day! Isn't that great?! My wife at that time was difficult enough to get along with, and this really wasn't going to help.

I called the district attorney a few weeks ahead of time and asked what we needed to do to make this as painless as possible and for it to some day just "go away". He stated that he needed someone to admit to being the shooter, and they would get a bigger fine and longer probation. I talked to Bubba and Fred about it. Fred said that he would admit to being the shooter as he had shot first, even though Bubba actually killed the deer. (Hey…I just cut its throat....didn't want it to suffer.) I called the district attorney back and worked it all out over the phone prior to the court date.

We drive back to Cottle County for court and get money orders to pay the court costs as that was what we were told to do. We go to the court house; it is an old 1930's building, four stories tall, (I think). It looked like it could use some paint; no elevator, stairs only and looked like it was built when Charles Goodnight was doing his cattle drives.

We go in and find the first floor hallway was lined with people, sitting and standing everywhere. I find the District Attorney's office and introduce ourselves. He was a very friendly fellow, and he thanked us for our cooperation. He found our paperwork and told us to wait in the hallway as court would begin in about twenty minutes.

As we sat in the old church pew style benches in the hallway, I looked at the hardwood floors that were devoid of stain and was showing years and years of wear. I wondered what kind of stories this old building could tell us.

Bubba was cooperative and well-behaved, much to my surprise. They still allowed smoking in this court house and at one end of the hall, close to the stairs was a gentleman wearing dress pants and a white dress shirt. He appeared to be about sixty-five years of age or better, with balding and graying hair. The guy was hovering over the ashtray, chain smoking As fast as he could smoke one cigarette, he would light another off it. I elbowed Bubba and Fred and said, "I wonder what that guy did? He's chain smoking like he's a nervous wreck."

In about fifteen minutes, an officer walked up to the chain smoker and said, "It's time to open the court and get busy, Your Honor." Your Honor grudgingly pulled a tie out of his pocket and began tying it on as someone helped him with his jacket. Up the stairs he went, followed by us and fifty other people. We filled the small court room which had folding chairs, the Judge's podium up front and a couple of other desks. The last person to enter the room was the only black person there, maybe the only one I had seen in town. The deputies brought him in, handcuffed and leg shackled, wearing a black and white striped prison suit. The once white stripes had turned gray with age.

When everyone got into the room, the Judge stretched his neck, looked to the back of the room and shouted, "Cooter! (I made up this name). Aren't you supposed to be fixing Miss Dessy's Cadillac?"

A young fellow with a ball cap on his head, covered in grease and with three wrenches and a red rag hanging out of his pant's pocket answered, "Yes, Sir, Your Honor."

"Then get your butt over there and fix her car! You and me will work this out later!" the Judge said.

"Yes, Sir, Your Honor," Cooter said as he zipped out the door,

The District Attorney spoke loudly to the Judge and asked, "Your Honor, I have three gentlemen here from East Texas, may we run them ahead of everyone else as they have a long drive back home?"

"Sure, no problem. Y'all come up here," the Judge said.

The District Attorney laid out our paperwork and had us look it over to make sure everything was correct. Mine and Fred's was correct. Bubba pointed out an error on his.

"Thank you very much for showing us that. If we hadn't corrected it, we couldn't have charged you with anything," the District Attorney said.

Bubba looked at me and Fred and mouthed 'WTF'. As the corrections were made on Bubba's paperwork, the Judge called our names as we stood in front of him. He called Bubba's name and said, "Bubba? Huh? East Texas, it figures!" The Judge read our charges, we pled guilty with Fred being the shooter. More paperwork was prepared, and the fines and penalties were read. A few thousand dollars and all three of us were placed on twelve months of probation and a year without hunting or fishing licenses.

As they dotted all the "I's" and crossed all the "T's", the Judge called us up to the bench and said, "Shooting deer at night! You boys don't get caught doing this again! I hate putting on this tie. Next time, y'all are here, call me. We'll drink a beer and shoot deer and y'all won't get in trouble!" Then he high-fived Bubba!

We thanked the Judge and shook his hand before leaving the Court Room. The District Attorney excused himself and had us follow him to his office. He made a phone call to the Game Wardens in Quanah who had our guns. He gave them our names and asked that they return our guns to us if we would come by and pick them up. (They could have legally kept them if they wanted to do so). I figured that my 30-06 was rusted and pitted by now since the night they took them it was raining and snowing, and we had not wiped them down before being confiscated. But to our surprise they were returned to us cleaned and oiled! The Game Warden said, "Don't let this deter you from coming back out here to hunt."

I've never been there again—-to hunt!

TIM & THE TORNADO (Toe-nae-doe)

I worked with a fellow, we'll call him, "Tim". We worked for the GMC dealer in Tyler, in the body shop ('nuff said). Tim had a bit of a speech impediment, not making fun, you just need to know this to understand and appreciate the story.

Tim lived in Pine Mills, North of Hawkins a few miles. One Spring, a tornado ripped through Pine Mills. The guys and me at work were concerned about Tim. We finally heard from him late the next day after the tornado. My buddy, Jason and I decided to go check on Tim after work and see if he needed anything.

Tim lived in an old trailer house out in the country. I had been there before, but Jason had not. I told Jason that he might not be able to tell what was blown in by the tornado and what was already there prior to the storm.

When we got to the Pine Mills Community, we could see twisted oak trees, roof blown off houses, barns flattened and all sort of destruction. When we pulled up at Tim's trailer, we could see his trailer was blown off its blocks and tilted on its side at a forty-five-degree angle. Tim was reattaching his satellite dish to a fence post and attempting to adjust it. We got out and greeted Tim, "Howdy, Tim! Are you alright?" I asked.

"Yeah, I'm fine. Y'all come on in. The electricity just came back on, and westlin' is coming on WWE!" Tim said.

Jason and I just looked at each other and followed Tim into his somewhat unlevel trailer house. As we walkin in, I noticed that all the windows were blown out and the floor looked like a fun house at a County Fair. It was buckled and wavy and the whole house tilted North! We sat down on the couch which felt like a recliner, as Tim propped up the T.V. so it wouldn't slide off the shelf. As Tim fiddles with the T.V., I asked the question, "Tim, shouldn't you try to put something over the windows and level your house back up?"

"I'll do it tomorrow. I gotta watch westlin'," he said.

"Is your little boy OK?" Jason asked.

"Yeah, he's OK. I was asleep on the couch when the storm hit. He's only three, but he woke me up. I couldn't get my shoes on—-guess I shouldn't have drunk the beers. I opened the funt doe (front door) and looked in the eye of the toe-nae doe!" Tim said. Tim had a big gash on his forehead between his eyes.

Jason asked, "What happened to your head?"

"When I opened the doe a shingle from the neighbor's house hit me and knocked me down," Tim said. "So, me and my boy laid on the flow (floor) and dug our fingers into the carpet. I told my boy to hold on we gotta' ride this thing out!"

After a little bit of watching wrestling, we made our way outside to survey the damage. We walked past a huge set of concrete steps turned upside down. "Damn! Look at this mess," Jason said.

"Dat already done before the storm," Tim replied.

Jason looked at a stock trailer laying on its side and asked, "Was that already like that before the storm?"

"No, the storm did that," Tim said.

Barn tin, wire and all sorts of debris was strewn across the pasture. We walked out to where the hog pen used to be. Posts were gone, wire was gone, the hog shed was gone. There was only an outline of the shed left on the ground. Laying in the middle of what used to be the hog shed was a huge hog, probably four hundred pounds. It appeared he had been killed by the tornado. We walked over the to the hog and Jason made the comment, "Dang, Tim! Your hog's dead!"

"He's not dead. That's Norm. Norm thinks he's in his house," Tim said as he gave Norm a kick and the huge hog grunted!

As Jason and I were leaving, we met a Channel 7 news van. When I got home, I turned on the T.V. to watch the news. Sure enough, as the news lady reported about the tornado, there was Tim in the background, dragging brush and debris. He was wearing his company shirt, blue jean shorts, a greasy ball cap and some cowboy boots, two sizes too big. They stopped him for an interview. "Pardon me, Sir. Did you see what happened?" the lady asked. "Yeah, I did, Tim said.

The Rest is History!

Jason & The Fiddle Faddle

My dear friend, Jason has more stories than I can pack into three books! Maybe, someday, we can make that happen.

One day at work, our boss, Carl Owens, brought in a box of Fiddle Faddle and left it for us to eat. Fiddle Faddle, folks, is like Cracker Jacks on steroids!! My buddy, Jason, tried some and immediately fell in love!

"Where do you get this stuff?" he asked.

"Carl gets it at Sam's Club," I said.

"I've got to have some! This stuff is GREAT!" he said.

The next week, Jason comes to me and asks, "You think Carl will get me a box of that Fiddle Faddle next time he goes to Sam's?"

"I'm sure he will," I replied.

"I've been trying for a week to get some," he said.

"What seems to be the problem?" I asked.

"Well, I went to Sam's and got a box of Fiddle Faddle—-that's all I wanted. I got to the checkout and the lady asked for my Sam's card. I didn't know I needed a Sam's card, and I didn't want to give forty dollars for a card just to get a box of Fiddle Faddle. So, I just handed her the Fiddle Faddle and walked out."

"My cousin told me that he had a Sam's card, and I could use it. A few days later, I borrowed his card and went back to Sam's, grabbed a box of Fiddle Faddle as that's all I wanted. I could taste it already as I walked up to the checkout. I put it on the counter and handed the lady my Sam's card. She scanned the card and asked if I would like to renew my card. It was expired!!! I looked at her, then looked at the Fiddle Faddle, then looked at the twenty dollars I was holding in my hand. I started to throw the twenty dollars down and run for it with the Fiddle Faddle, but I didn't. I handed her the Fiddle Faddle, took the card and walked out. I stood in the parking lot for a while, watching people go in and out, I started to get one person's attention…you know, like…*'Pssst, hey here's a twenty-dollar bill. Will you get me some Fiddle Faddle? (in a whisper).'* I felt like a teenager at a liquor store. But I didn't because I was afraid they would think I was crazy and call the cops," Jason said.

I don't think Jason has gotten any Fiddle Faddle to this day. I should go buy him some; now that I think about it.

RED AINSWORTH BARBER SHOP ANTICS

If you've never been to a small town, barber shop—-then Brother, I pity you! It's more fun than Disney World!

My dear friend and Masonic Brother, Red Ainsworth, cut my hair for over twenty years before he passed. He was a character, to put it mildly… yeah, y'all know what I'm saying…those who knew him.

Red, who had become follicly challenged, (as one of my M/C brothers calls it—-thanks for the phrase, Cracker) kept his hair buzzed off and wore glasses which he would peer over the tops of to look at you when trying to make a point during any one of his conversations that could and sometimes would turn in to something like a university professor's lecture. Red was never short on words, always had an answer for everything and a funny story at any given moment. Most of his haircuts took a littler longer than normal because of these great conversations and semi-lectures. I loved it!

Anything from politics, religion, gardening, fishing, mechanics, hunting, to the latest science and technology—-Red could talk about anything and knew what he was talking about. During the haircut procedure, he would comb and clip and buzz the patron's hair, in-between he would pause to address his audience-in-waiting. He would point his clippers at them and peer over his glasses to make sure they were paying attention and getting the point.

I'm sure first-time patrons didn't know what to make of the whole thing, but one thing's for sure—-they always came back.

One Saturday morning, I hurried down to Red's to get a haircut and found that the place was full already. Eight or ten people were waiting, and one was in the chair. When I opened the door, Red said, "Come on in here boy, join the fun."

I sat down next to another Mason Brother, Jim Long. Jim is an old Marine with a deep, bass voice. I asked him, " Brother Jim, have I missed anything this morning?"

"Damn! Socrates himself doesn't stand a chance in here this morning!" Jim said.

Another time, Red had Terry Montgomery in the chair talking politics and buzzing away. Well, two or three of us got Red stirred up about the current President at that time. He would talk loudly, point his clippers at us, peer over his glasses like a wild man and then buzz and snip and cut like crazy! All the while, Terry was afraid to move, he was drawn up in a knot and had a funny look on his face. He was frozen and not saying anything (which is unusual for Terry). We were laughing and having a big time as we stoked the fires that caused Red to go into overdrive! When Red was finished, he spun Terry around and he leapt out of the chair and said, "Dammit! Y'all better not ever do that shit again!

Oh, Yeah! We just laughed harder!

Red had an old fellow in the chair one day and Red asked him, " George, isn't this your and your wife's anniversary?"

"Yeah, we've been married thirty good years," George said. Well, I said thirty *good* years—-we've been married fifty!"

For every young man getting married, Red always had some great words to reassure them of their decision. He would ask them, "Son, do you know the difference between a wedding and a hanging?"

The answer from the young man was always, "No". Red would always calmly say, "A hanging is more humane!" But Red always reassured them of how great marriage was.

There are many, many stories which Red told that I can't put in this book. I can't tell them here because everyone wouldn't understand them. But hit me up and I will be glad to tell them, or if you have some stories about him, please let me know.

Red was a great guy and a solid Brother. He is missed.

P.S. I'm sure Red will make another appearance in this book before I'm finished.

BLACK POWDER IN THE BODY SHOP

My buddy, Jason—-yes, Fiddle Faddle Jason, is a builder of homemade cannons on occasions. In order to fire these cannons, you need some black powder just like the old muzzle loaders use.

We were working for the GMC dealer at the time, and we had a helper named Danny. Now, Danny is kinda' short and wide (you know I love you, Danny), has an accent that is a combination of East Texas and Alabama. Danny is one of the most likeable fellows you will ever meet. He smiles and laughs all of the time. Danny was not the fastest helper we ever had, but probably the smartest. He talked the boss into hiring him a helper to do his work! Yes, the helper got a helper! I never saw anything like it. That's another story also.

Back to the black powder. Jason brought a little bit of black powder to work with him and made a small pile of it out in the shop. The pile was probably one-third the size of a coke can. Jason rounded the pile up, made a neat little mound of it and then pulled out his lighter. We were all watching except for the boss, Pat. He was in the office.

Me, Danny, Tim (yes, Tornado Tim) and Jason gathered around the small mound of black powder, contemplating how to go about setting it off. (Hey Folks, if you don't know about body shop guys, we're outlaws, a cross between construction worker, oilfield hands and prison inmates).

Jason and I knew that black powder explodes on point of ignition. It doesn't' sizzle or run a trail of sparks and then explode. It blows up! Jason was looking for something long to light with in order to set it off, when Danny says, "Give me that lighter and let's do this!"

Jason hands Danny the lighter. Danny is bending over the pile of powder trying to make a small narrow trail about ten inches long. After several seconds, Jason says, "Are you going to light that shit or just fuck around all day?!"

At that point, still bending over the pile of black powder, Danny lights the trail of powder which he has so neatly laid out.

WHOOM!

Danny with Bic lighter in his outstretched arm goes up in a flash of fire and smoke, just like a magic show—-except louder! Danny stands up in the aura of smoke that has filled the shop. He turns to us with half his mustache burnt off; half his face, powder burned; right arm red; hair singed; clothes on fire and smoking and calmly says, "Good thing I'm fast!"

Tim runs over to Danny and starts patting him all over his chest and belly, hollering, "You on fire, Danny! You on fire!"

Jason and I were way too busy laughing to be of any assistance. Danny's eyes are a little crossed, and he is still gripping the lighter, while Tim puts out his fire. The smoke rolled up to the rafters in the tall ceiling of the body shop, and the manager came running out a few minutes later.

"What's going on out here?" he asked.

"Danny set off some of my black powder," Jason said.

Pat just shook his head and turned to go back to his office.

We inspected Danny a little closer once we contained ourselves. His right hand and arm were devoid of hair and were bright red. His shirt was half-scorched, half his mustache was gone as well as most of one eyebrow, the right side of his face was powder burned and the right side of his hair was singed. He looked like a cartoon character that had been in an explosion.

He still attests to this day that it would have been worse, had he not been so fast and relied on his catlike reflexes to avoid the blast. Hmmmm… go figure.

SHOOTOUT AT THE BLUE BONNET INN
RED AINSWORTH, EYE WITNESS

I have thought long and hard about this story and I am going to reword it a little, but for the most part—-it's spot on.

Brother Red's barber shop was—-is—-right next door to the Blue Bonnet Inn Motel in Hawkins. Many years ago, there was a shootout in the parking lot that involved several individuals. The T.V. interview with Brother Red is the focus of this short story. (The interview they would not put on air).

The news crews swarmed the parking lot of the Blue Bonnet Inn and then made their way over to Red's barber shop after the fracas was over and cleaned up.

As the reporter and camera man focused on Red, the question was asked, "Mr. Ainsworth, did you see what happened, Sir?"

"Yeah, I did," Red said.

He explained what he saw, "This one was here, that one was there, those two were over yonder. This one shot that one, that one shot those two and ran over there and then got shot by that one, and so forth and so on." The news crew listened intently and with awe as they got this firsthand, eye witness account of the murders. When Red finished his elaborate account of the incident he said, "But they're some damn fools!"

As the camera rolled, the reporter asked, "Why do you say that, Mr. Ainsworth?"

"Because the cops say that there were still bullets in all the guns and there were still sorry mother f—-kers that needed killing!" Red said as he peered over his glasses and pointed his barber's clippers at the camera. Then he topped it off with, "Put that in your damned report, because I don't think you want to hear the truth!" Red said, as the reporter's mouth dropped open and he started making a cutting motion across his throat to the camera man, who immediately tilted their camera to the floor.

Gotta love Red! He always told the truth! Even if you didn't want to hear it.

Once again, Brother Red is missed!

VOODOO IN THE OIL PATCH

What would East Texas stories be without a little Louisiana Voodoo thrown in?

My buddy, Dennis (not my brother, but my Masonic Brother) was working as a rig hand in Louisiana many years ago and told me this story that I thought was noteworthy.

Dennis said that every morning, he and three other hands would get up and head to the drilling rig which was several miles out in the Louisiana backwoods and swamps. Every day they would pass an old shack down one of the sandy dirt roads that led to the rig Outside this shack there was usually an old woman with long, stringy, gray hair. She had a slightly bent body, and she held a stick which she used as a cane. The rig hands that rode with Dennis referred to her as Miss Marie, the Voodoo Lady. As they would pass by, stirring up dust on the dirt road, Miss Marie would point and wave her stick at them and curse. Dennis asked what that was all about, and one of the hands explained that evidently, Miss Marie didn't like them driving down this road. After several days of passing Miss Marie's shack and lots of pointing and cursing, she evidently decided to put her trade to work.

One morning, upon reaching the stretch of road in front of Miss Marie's shack, they could see that in the sandy road were several effigies and odd symbols drawn in the sand in the middle of the road and strange stick figure or signs hung along the ditches.

Two of the hands screamed, "Hawwww, stop this truck!" "Lord, let me out of here!" they said.

These two hands were big, tough, strong oilfield rig hands. They had rather fight than eat. They would wade through wild cats to fight a buzz saw. But..(yes, but) they were scared to death of the signs and effigies left by the Voodoo Lady. They jumped out of the truck as it slid to a stop. They refused to get back in or go any further down this road.

"We've got an oilwell to drill, boys! I don't have time for this foolishness!" the boss told them. But no matter how much reason, demanding or begging the boss did, they refused to go any further.

"That drilling rig is going to blow up or sink into the swamp or something bad is going to happen," one of the hands said. Those two hands walked back to town, rather than go anywhere near the cursed rig or the road. Dennis and the other hand pulled up on location and explained what had happened and now they were two men short, with a deadline to meet.

The big boss rounded everybody up and threatened them. "I don't want to hear any more talk about Voodoo around this rig or this crew! You boys from Texas better keep your mouths shut. You don't understand how things work down here in Louisiana. Folks take Voodoo very seriously, and whether you believe it or not, they do!" he said.

The well was drilled, the rig didn't sink or blow up, the two hands that quit, didn't come back. But, as a coon ass friend of mine says about Voodoo, bad luck and spirits...

...YOU NEVER KNOW!

HILLBILLIES & MEXICANS

All of my life, at one time or another, people have referred to me as a "hillbilly". Even as a child, I preferred to go barefoot and wear nothing but my blue jeans as I roamed around the farm among all the critters. Most of the time, I liked the company of the animals rather than people or the solace of the woods or fields (sometime, I still have these preferences).

Being raised way out in the country, by country parents has its benefits even though some people seem to think this is a disadvantage to modern knowledge. But I'll put my country education and raising up against college knowledge any day.

In the biker world or M/C (motorcycle club) world, everyone has a road name, so inevitably mine is "Hillbilly". It was years of this tag being put on me that landed me with a road name like "Hillbilly". I wear it with pride. People ask how I got the name. The stories tend incidents are too numerous to tell, but I will relate one in particular that involves my buddy, Bubba! Yeah! Bubba again.

Me and Bubba were down in South Texas on the Mexican border visiting a friend. We'll call him, "Jake". Jake took us to a party with some of his friends. All the dudes at this party were Mexicans. Me, Jake and Bubba were the only three white dudes there. No problem, just pointing this out.

They had a huge brick, open top, firepit with all kinds of meat cooking on it. Music was playing, beer was flowing, lots of laughing. We were having a great time. Bubba and I seemed to be the center of attention most of the evening. Everyone was curious about these white guys from East Texas. Later that night, they broke out a bottle of Tequila, and the music was turned down. Everyone turned their attention to us and three of our hosts who were pouring shots of Tequila for us. We toasted and shot the Tequila without salt or lime (the way I like it). We drank half the bottle or more and then they broke out a bottle of Mezcal.

Everyone got quiet again, the music was turned down, our hosts poured only two shot glasses of the Mezcal, double shot glasses this time. As soon as it was poured, Bubba and I snatched them up and downed them without making a face or expression and then said, "Ahhh, let's have another one!" Our party hosts looked at Jake and in an angry tone, said, "Jake you lied to us!

"What are you talking about?" asked Jake.

"You told us that your friends were rednecks from East Texas. These are f—-king hillbillies!!" one shouted and then died laughing as everyone cheered and turned the music up, so the party could begin again. We had a great time! FYI—Bubba is half-Mexican so there was two-and-a-half white guys there.

BUBBA & ME in OLD MEXICO

My buddy, Bubba and I have made several trips across the border into Old Mexico. I'll hit on some highlights because anytime Bubba is around there is no such thing as a dull time.

We crossed the border into Matamoras, Mexico with wives and children. We walked across as we had done several times before. The wives and daughters wanted to shop at the market and some silver jewelry stores. We went from store to store making our way to the market. We had been advised by a friend who lived there that we should only ride taxis or buses that were owned by the Garcias. When we were tired of walking, we caught a bus that had "Garcia" written on its side, It dropped us off in front of a store owned by the Garcias, imagine that!

The jewelry store owner and employees were more than accommodating, especially with three or four women and several girls looking at jewelry. As the women shopped, Bubba and I hung out at one end of the counter. The store owner came over and asked us if we wanted a beer! "Well! Of course!" said Bubba. The guy opens up the frig behind the counter and pulls out two Coronas, opens them for us and goes back to tend to the women. I'm not a big beer drinker, but Bubba on the other hand—-Well, I'll just say the storekeeper just "screwed up". It was August and hot outside; the store was air-conditioned, and the store keeper was giving away free beer. Needless to say, after about the fifth or sixth beer, the store keeper stopped offering them. Bubba started asking for another every time he finished one.

The ladies and daughters bought a good amount of jewelry, and the store keeper was probably trying to calculate whether or not he made a profit after Bubba got through with the free beer.

The ladies and girls were making rounds in the market area, so Bubba and I spotted a cantina and strolled inside. We pulled up stools at the bar and ordered more beers. There wasn't anyone there except the bar tender, me and Bubba and one other Mexican dude sitting at the bar. I went to the restroom and was in a stall getting rid of some of the beer, when I heard the door open, and someone came in. I promise you that I am aware of my surroundings at all times. Especially, when I'm in Matamoras, Mexico. Whoever came in, did not come in to take care of business, because I could hear them shuffling around by the door instead of occupying a bathroom stall or urinal. So, having only a pocket knife, I pulled it out and opened it as I zipped up and turned to exit the stall, expecting to have to defend myself against a Mexican bandit, I confront what is the bathroom attendant holding towels and hand soap for my use! Well, who would have thought we were in such a classy joint? When I realize what the dude's gig really is, I close my knife and stop pointing it at him He was as surprised as I was. I washed and tipped the guy a dollar for handing me soap and a towel. I did not tell Bubba what had just happened…I really didn't think it was necessary.

A few minutes later, Bubba goes into the restroom. A few seconds later, the dude at the end of the bar goes in after Bubba. I'm sitting, trying to decipher the Spanish Channel on T.V. and checking out the bar décor. Now, it's sometimes not unusual for Bubba to take a long bathroom break, so I really wasn't' thinking much of it when Bubba had been gone for several minutes. However, after a while, I started getting concerned. Bubba finally comes back to the bar, and I ask him if he's alright.

"Yeah, I'm alright. I heard someone come in after me, so I stayed in the stall waiting on them to leave. I thought I was gonna get jacked. I waited and waited, but they never left. So, I looked around for a weapon. Nothing! Nothing at all, not even a pocket knife! I bust out of the stall like a mad man ready to fight! And there's this dude standing there holding towels and soap!" he says.

At this point I'm laughing at him, of course. "You asshole what are you laughing at?" he asked me.

"Same thing happened to me, except I got a knife," I said. "Did you tip the dude?" I asked.

"Tip him?" Bubba asked.

'Yeah, tip him, he's a bathroom attendant, that's his job." I said.

"No, I didn't tip him! I'm not tipping somebody for scaring the hell out of me!" Bubba said.

MATAMORAS CONTINUES

Another time, much like the previous story, we were in Matamoras with our families and friends having a great time. After a day of shopping and Curious Bubba antics, we stopped to eat. We again found a cantina restaurant that had the coldest A.C. and the coldest Tecate on a hot, August day.

Between me and Bubba and our friend, Jake, wives, children and our children's friends, we were a party of about twenty-one all together. We ate fajitas with homemade tortillas and goat cheese (some of the best I have ever eaten), beer, drinks, shots of Tequila, lots of fun and laughter. Bubba and I were going to split the bill and buy for everyone. The bill came and I showed it to Bubba…$1,120.00. I did a double take and then I made the assumption that it was in pesos. I was correct. But I didn't tell Bubba. I showed him the bill. Curious Bubba looked like I had just run over his foot with a steam roller. His mouth was open, his eyes almost crossed, he couldn't breathe. He snatched the check out of my hand and headed toward the waiter before I could stop him. He was pointing at the check and pointing at the table we were at and shaking his head and jabbering so fast the waiter couldn't understand him.

The waiter took the check and explained that it was in pesos, and if he had America dollars it was $120.00. What a great relief! Bubba came back and melted into his seat. The sudden scare had killed his buzz. He explained to me what the deal was.

"I know," I said.

"What??!! Why didn't you tell me before I made a fool of myself?" Bubba asked

"Well Bubba, I thought it was funny and plus you didn't give me time to explain," I said.

"Good grief! That like to a made me sick!" Bubba said.

We paid the bill and took enough leftovers home to eat for a second night. Great place, great food! I think the name was Bigo's Restaurant and Cantina.

It was getting dark and walking back down the streets and alleys of a border town can be daunting . We had our wives and several children to keep track of not to mention one Curious Bubba.

As we walked, Bubba began to clutch his stomach, I could hear it rumble. He would walk and grab his stomach and do some kind of bizarre dance, much like an African Witch Doctor would dance. Every alleyway that we encountered, Bubba would peer down it, into the darkness as he held his stomach, contemplating relief.

"I wouldn't go down any of these alleys if I were you, Bubba," I warned him. "And I'm not going with you," I added.

We walked as fast as we could get our herd of twenty-one kids and adults to move. Bubba was leading the way holding his stomach, bent over like a chimpanzee. As we got closer and closer to the border crossing, Bubba was twisting and shaking like he was Elvis on a Vegas stage. Suddenly, there was a light at the end of the tunnel. A three-story restaurant and store owned by the Garcias which was still open. Bubba sprinted to the front door, flung it open and rushed in, pushing people out of his way. We stood on the street and waited.

It was kind of a fancy restaurant. We had eaten there before. From the street, we could see through the big plate glass window people dining on the third floor. Suddenly, we see Bubba dashing across the restaurant, holding his stomach with one hand and the other hand outstretched in front of him like he was carrying a football. He dodged tables, shoved waiters out of the way, and I think he leapt over some potted plants before disappearing into a restroom. We were stunned at first as we didn't expect to see that. We had figured he would stop on the first floor at the General Store restroom. Then we all started laughing. After several long minutes, we see Bubba casually walking across the dining room like Fonzey and talking to the patrons and waiters (as he will do). He comes out the front door and rejoins us. We start laughing again.

"What's so funny? I was in a nine-line bind. I liked to not made it!" he said.

"Why didn't you go to the one on the first floor?" I asked.

"Well, I knew where the one in the restaurant was, and I didn't have time to stop and ask where the others were. So, I made a run for it!" he said.

SABINE RIVER BIGFOOT

Anyone who knows me, knows I am all about Bigfoot. I have read and studied everything I can about the subject. I have found footprints and had personal sightings, myself. Sometimes I joke about it, but I am quite serious about the mystery they call Bigfoot, Sasquatch, Skookum, etc., etc.

I can talk about it extensively to anyone who cares to listen. My friend, Chris, who was working with me at the time, enjoyed listening to my ramblings about the elusive creature, but he was on the fence about believing in the subject. He hadn't seen or heard one but didn't rule out the possibility of its existence.

I had told him about my buddy, Bubba and his brothers who had found a dead deer during bow season, down on the Sabine River. It looked to be only a day-old dead with an arrow stuck in it! The next morning, they go back to examine the carcass, and it was gone! Not drug off, no drag marks, no scattered body parts or blood—-just gone! Like something had picked it up and carried it away. It was nowhere to be found. It was on their property, and the deer was past the point of being edible—-October gets warm in Texas.

One night, Chris was having some family issues. So, he got in his truck and drove down to the Sabine River Wildlife Refuge or Game Management Area North of Lindale. It was a dark night, stars were out, no one else in that area of the river or in the woods. There weren't any vehicles around, and it's a pretty good drive off the main road.

It was around 11 p.m. and Chris sits down on his tailgate pondering the current problems that plague his life. He lays back and looks up at the stars. It's calm and quiet, until a small rock hits the side of his pickup. TINK! He sits up quickly and looks around in the darkness. He doesn't see or hear anything, so he lays back down to gaze at the stars, He shrugs it off and blames it on me and my stories of rock throwing Big Foots. That what it is, he thinks, just my imagination and Ron's stories working on my brain.

Then, in a few minutes, …TINK! Another rock hits his truck. He pops up like a jack-in-the-box and grabs a flashlight. He sweeps the woods and brush with his light like it's a prison break—-but NOTHING! He sees and hears nothing, no kind of sounds—-just quiet. With light and shotgun in hand, he nervously surveys the woods one more time as he gets in the cab and fires up the engine, throws it in gear and spins the tires as he leaves the river bottom in a cloud of dust, depriving the Big Foots of their entertainment.

The next day he relays the story to me, blaming me for putting the thoughts in his head. But he is unable to explain the rock throwing, and he wasn't parked under any trees.

Be aware of your surroundings in the Sabine River Bottom!

THE ROUGAROU & IZZY

For the ones of you that don't know about the Rougarou, it's a Louisiana Version of Big Foot to some people. Some say a Sasquatch-type creature, some say a werewolf; some say a shape shifter or human by day and Rougarou during full moons. Whatever this hairy, mythical beast is, it is deeply rooted in the minds and mysteries of Louisiana. They believe when this creature howls and roams the swamps, bayous and thickets, that it is searching for souls to take as well as your body.

There was this happy-go-lucky guy who I worked with. He was from South Louisiana, we'll call him "Izzy". He was medium build, stocky shoulders, strong and tough. He had coal black hair and beard, olive skin and he was always laughing, joking and aggravating people just for entertainment. He walked like he didn't have a care in the world and everyday was sunshine. He wore sunglasses most all the time and was a very hard worker. He was one of our sand blasters (a very tough job).

Izzy came zipping by me one day with his normal swagger and carefree smile, and I asked, "Hey Izzy, do you believe in the Rougarou?"

Izzy stopped in mid-swagger, slowly reached up and pulled off his sunglasses, looked me in the eye and in a slow, low tone asked me, "What's a guy like you know about the Rougarou?"

I replied, "Well, I've always heard about them and was just curious what you knew or thought since you're from South Louisiana."

Izzy was still holding his shades and looked left and right and then all around to see if anyone was listening or watching us. Then he looked back at me and said, " No, I don't' believe in any of that stuff or the Voodoo, but you never know!" His normal, happy composure had become solemn, and his smile had become a face of stone. He slowly put his sunglasses back on and walked away. He didn't look at me or speak to me for two weeks after that.

This was evidently a touchy subject which he took seriously even if he had said otherwise. Something about my question spooked him or brought back some memories. I'm not sure what!

After a couple of weeks, he approached me and told me that his dad was very superstitious, and that one time when he was a child they were driving to see some of "our people", he called them. A black cat crossed the road in front of them. His Father stopped the car, went home and never drove down that particular road again. I'm not sure, but maybe he felt it was some sort of bad luck or something for me to ask about the Rougarou. I never mentioned it again.

ROUGAROU & THE OIL PATCH

My buddy, Dennis, also had an encounter with some believers in the Rougarou. This is the same crew that had the run in with the old Voodoo woman on the dirt road. They also got spooked when the moon was full. They were working night shift down in the swamp on a drilling rig.

Being a young deck hand and the lowest on the totem pole, Dennis had to fetch and get whatever he was told to do. One night, when the full moon rose above the swamps and cypress of Louisiana, the rig hands' talk turned to the Rougarou. These big, tough, rough necks, who would wade through wild cats to fight a buzz saw, became nervous and jumpy. The howl of a coyote got their attention, and one hand suggested that it was the Rougarou wandering through the swamp, searching for souls to take. Dennis being curious as always and asked questions about the Rougarou, so that he could be clear about what he might be dealing with. One hand told him that it looked like a man, covered with hair, with a tail like a wolf and a long snout and pointed ears. It could howl like a wolf and came out on moonlit nights. Dennis asked what they would do if such a creature approached the rig. One hand said that he was going to climb to the top of the drilling rig, as high as he could go, "And I hope it gets one of y'all and not me!" he told them, seriously without any hesitation or humor in his voice.

So, as long as the moon was full, whenever someone had to get off the rig or platform to fetch something they always sent Dennis. Everyone else would stay up on the rig and just watch as he retrieved the needed tool or supplies, waiting and watching to see if the Rougarou was going to snatch his next victim.

Needless to say, my friend lived to tell this story…

…But…you never know….!!

BIG FOOT—-SEEING IS BELIEVING—-BUT NOT ALWAYS!

My friend, Dennis in the aforementioned story, is about eighteen years older than me. A serious, no nonsense kind of guy. Solid in what he believes or doesn't believe. Anytime the subject of Big Foot or Sasquatch came up in conversation, Dennis would refuse to talk about it or entertain the idea of such a creature. He would even get mad if you wanted to discuss it. It wasn't even a joke to him. His theory was that he had been in the woods all of his life and hunted day and night and had never, never seen anything like these creatures. So therefore, they did not exist, since he had not seen one. This is a firm stance that many outdoors men take on the subject. I'm not here to convince anyone, nor am I *trying* to convince anyone, but if you don't believe something exists, then it's easy not to look for it or notice it. It simply does not exist. If you've read my first book, then you know where I stand on the subject of Big Foot. I am a believer and a knower, but I really hope no one ever proves their existence. Life is more interesting with a few mysteries.

My dear friend, Dennis, knew how I enjoyed talking about Big Foot, even though I never mentioned it around him, and he had not heard all of my encounters at this time.

It was Spring time in early May. Dennis and I headed to Mena, Arkansas to scout out some places in the mountains to go bear hunting. Arkansas has more, black bear than any other state in the Union. The Ouachita Mountains around the Mena area are beautiful. The rivers are clean and rocky and there are hundreds of thousands or millions of acres of National Forest to hunt and it's a Sportsman's Paradise, just like they advertise. If you're driving or hiking the mountains in Southwest Arkansas, you don't know when you're in Oklahoma or Arkansas. The state line runs through the mountains and the mountain range runs East and West from Arkansas to Oklahoma. These are the Ouachita and Kiamichi Mountains. Lots of Big Foot sightings and activity in those mountains in both states…just saying.

Dennis and I drove Northwest of Mena and started our scouting on a gravel road around Eagleton community. We would drive and stop every now and then, get out and walk up and down creeks and streams, looking for signs of bear and deer. After about two hours of driving these mountain gravel roads, we had not seen any other vehicles, which is not unusual. With the aid of a National Forest map, we followed roads and trails. We turned off onto a somewhat unused overgrown trail that was on the map but didn't appear to be traveled or kept up by the National Forest authorities. It was a trail going along the top of a small mountain range. It was just like a trail in a pasture, two lines in the grass where your tires go and ankle-deep grass and weeds in-between. We drove along the trail with the landscape fairly open on both sides until we came to about one hundred feet of road sloping down to the tree line of pine and oak. We drove slowly, trying to look around us and looking at the trail ahead for any sign of scat.

We noticed some scat on the trail ahead and got out to examine it and to try to determine if it was from a bear or some other animal and to possibly determine what it had been eating. Upon close examination, we determined it was bear scat. On the edge of the scat (which I think we determined was probably less than a day old) was the impression of a toe. Yes, a toe print, a very human-looking toe print.

I pointed out the toe print to Dennis, but I did not say "human-looking" although I was thinking it.

I said, "Look at this toe print," and pointed at it. Dennis went from bent over observation to crouching and looking, as I did. We were both silent, not a sound, not a movement, only stares at the human-looking toe print in the middle of the Ouachita Mountains in a pile of scat. With one motion, Dennis stood up, turned down the trail and walked away. He continued to walk about fifty or eighty feet, stopped, lit a cigarette and observed his surroundings. I took one more look and then walked back to the driver's door. Dennis made his way back to the truck, and we began our journey again. There were at least ten or twelve minutes without conversation as we drove, which is unusual. I could tell that he was aggravated by the way he was puffing on his cig.

Then he spoke, "Ronald, you know how I feel about that subject. I think it's nonsense and there is no such thing. If you were to see one of these things, I'm not the person you want with you," he said. He was agitated and serious,

I didn't say anything Dennis," I replied.

"I know you didn't, but I know what you were thinking," he said.

What did it look like to you?" I asked.

"It looked like a human toe print," he replied.

"You're the perfect witness Dennis. You're a solid nonbeliever," I said. "If you did see one, would you believe what you saw?" I asked.

"There is no such thing, so I can't say that I would, he replied.

We drove another twenty or thirty minutes in silence and then resumed our normal conversation . Everything was back to normal, and I didn't make mention of the toe print again,

Another hour passed, and we found ourselves driving around a narrow mountain trail, winding around a ridge with sharp corners, drop offs to my left and a mountain going almost vertical to my right.

Many, many years of hunting and spending time with Dennis has made me well aware of his excellent sight and hearing. Especially, when it comes to being in the woods and hunting. If he said he heard something, then he heard it. Hunting at night, he has heard pigs and hogs two hundred yards away, and I thought "no way" because I didn't hear them. Then, all of the sudden, there they are. Time and again this has happened. The same with seeing and spotting animals at night or during the day. I told you that, to tell you this:

As we drove around that steep ridge, I was watching the narrow trail and looking at the drop off to my left as I drove. All of the sudden, Dennis yells, "STOP!" and racks a round into his pistol, as do I as soon as I stop. Dennis is not overly dramatic, and if he says we have a problem then, "WE HAVE A PROBLEM!"

I sit waiting for instruction as he stares up the mountain to his—-our—-right. He's left-handed and the pistol's barrel is resting on the open window pointing up the mountain. He said, "Back up, six feet."

I do as he asked. He is scanning the side of the mountain. He hasn't changed his line of sight since he yelled, "STOP!" He didn't need to look to chamber a round.

"I saw someone watching us," he said.

"Up there?" I asked.

"Yes, up there behind that scrub oak," he said and pointed up at a patch of scrub oak that looked to be about twelve or fourteen feet wide, maybe four foot tall and approximately one-hundred-eighty feet up an almost vertical mountainside that was dotted with tall pines and scrub oaks and a few boulders.

"We haven't seen any vehicles of any kind or people for two hours and no telling how many miles, Dennis," I said.

"I know, but there was someone up there watching us." he replied. "Maybe someone up here growing marijuana, " he said.

"Could be, but that's an almost impossible climb, it looks like to me. Maybe not impossible, but not very easy and if they were there, they couldn't get away without you seeing them," I said.

"I know it, but he's there, I saw him. I just don't know where he went. He ducked down behind the scrub oak, when I told you to stop," he said. "Back up some more," he said, eyes never leaving the side of the mountain.

We drove backwards and forwards, looking all over the side of the mountain. The area was open enough between the big pines and scattered brush and boulders, that you could see someone or something if it were to move or run away. Finally, after twenty or thirty minutes, we gave up and continued our journey once again.

"I don't know how he got away without me seeing him," Dennis kept saying.

Dennis is an excellent hunter and tracker. He has been all his life. He will rarely miss a shot or lose track of an animal even in difficult or harsh circumstances. I have all the confidence in the world when he says he saw something.

At this point, I am positive that Dennis had seen someone upon the side of the mountain even as impossible or improbable that it would seem, considering the landscape or at least the difficulty of an almost vertical mountainside.

"What did he look like?" I asked.

"He had a long, grayish black beard. All I could see was his eyes and nose and mouth," he replied.

"Did he have on a hat or cap? What color shirt?" I asked, thinking that at some point we might run across someone who fit the description on these trails and gravel roads.

"No. No cap or hat. His hair hung down on or past his shoulders, and his beard hung down to his chest. He was behind the brush, and I could only see him from his chest up. He had so much hair and such a big beard I couldn't see any clothes, just greyish, black hair," he said.

At that moment, my mind did a cartwheel. My friend, who is a nonbeliever and is certain that there is no such thing as Big Foot, had just seen a Big Foot! But because Big Foot doesn't exist, then the only logical explanation would be that it was somebody—-a human with long hair and beard, which made him appear devoid of clothing, who disappeared rapidly, making an escape in an impossible setting in the middle of the Ouachita Mountains.

I drove and pondered this, repeating in my mind everything that Dennis had said and recounting the setting, landscape and everything about the event. This happened some time round the Spring of 2012 on a clear, sunshiny day, northwest of Mena, Arkansas.

To this day, Dennis does not understand how that person managed to allude us on the side of a difficult to climb mountainside where no human should have been or had any reason to be there,

I've never told him my theory. If you see it, but don't believe it exists, then it must be something else, even if that something else doesn't make sense.

INSPECTOR GADGET

There is a dog that deserves honorable mention in this book. His name is Inspector Gadget. Gadget's owner, Jason, loves animals and takes excellent care of his dogs. But (yes, there's that "but" again), Mr. Gadget seemed to have a knack for getting hurt or getting into trouble, and he was an excellent escape artist. Gadget was part dachshund and who knows what else. Mr. Gadget looked more like a weasel or an otter than a dog. He was long and had the slinky body and short legs of a dachshund. He had a long tail, and his ears were shorter than most dachshund's ears. He was probably twice the size of an average dog of that breed. He was a goofy lookin' sight!

Jason kept his dog penned during the day while he was at work and turned him loose in the evenings. His need to be penned was because of a busy highway close by, and the fact that Mr. Gadget had begun a daily ritual of conscripting people's trash and garbage and bringing it home to be strewn about in Jason's yard, which he kept very, very tidy and well-groomed.

When running loose in the countryside, Mr. Gadget would hunt down, sniff out and find the most disgusting garbage and trash that he could find and bring it home with him. Jason would wake up to or come home to everything from dirty diapers to rotten, maggot-infested meat or any other unthinkable, unmentionable, discarded item that you can imagine. So, after several gut-wrenching trash details to clean his own yard, he decided to pen Mr. Gadget while he was at work or asleep. Oh, I forgot to mention that Mr. Gadget had come home more than once with his butt bleeding from being shot with birdshot (probably from tearing up someone's trash). So, for his own protection and Jason's sanity, Mr. Gadget was on a part-time jail program.

Jason decided to run an electric wire around the top of the dog pen to restrain Mr. Gadget and prevent further escapes. Being a DIY kinda' person, Jason made his own electric fence and plugged it straight into a 110-volt outlet. This worked for a day or two. Then, one day, Jason looked out the window in amazement as Mr. Gadget scaled the fence and became entangled in the electric wire and the fence. He twitched and jerked as 110-volt current flowed through him, His slinky body wriggled like a snake. But, before Jason could run outside and unplug the fence, Mr. Gadget summed all of his garbage-eating super strength and freed himself of the shockingly bleak situation. He powered through the pain of electric shock and continued to climb, determined to be a free-range trash hound. He leapt over the top of the fence, still twitching and smoking as he fled to pursue his desire for disgusting cuisine. He returned later with some unthinkable buffet.

Sometime after the electric fence episode, Mr. Gadget had a stroke. It was not determined if it was from the electricity or being shot again with birdshot or a combination. Maybe it was his dietary habits...I don't know. Anyway, the stroke didn't kill him, and he was back to normal except for his tongue hanging out of his mouth all the time. When he ate or drank or ran around, his tongue hung out. And since he was so short, his tongue drug the ground and stayed dirty all the time. This didn't seem to bother him, he had a palate that delighted in the obscure.

Jason likes to hunt for Indian arrow heads and he's good at it. He took Mr. Gadget with him one day, thinking Mr. Gadget would enjoy a run out in the wide-open spaces with no trash around to tear up.   Jason was north of Tyler, hunting for arrow heads. For several hours, he lost track of Mr. Gadget, who normally stayed close by when they were in unfamiliar territory. He couldn't find Mr. Gadget anywhere, and finally gave up the search and returned home. Home was thirty miles north of Tyler. After about three months, and no sign of Mr. Gadget, Jason figured he would never see him again. He thought perhaps a big cat or coyote had eaten him.

About this time, we were at work, looking at the newspaper and in the section where they feature a weekly ad for animals that need adopting from the pound was a picture of Mr. Gadget! Yes! Mr. Gadget was the "Pet of the Week"! They had changed his name to "Colton". "Colton's a Cutie", the caption under the picture read.

Jason said, "Will you look at this! Mr. Gadget is in jail at the dog pound, and he's up for adoption or else they will put him down. I guess I better go bail him out and take him home."

Jason bailed Mr. Gadget out of jail and took him home. He was lost south of Tyler and picked up by the dog catcher on the north side of Tyler close to Highway 14 which would be the way he would go home; straight down Highway 14 and then north to Hawkins. He was headed home——just taking his time.

I told Jason that he had probably found two or three new homes, but when he started dragging up trash and all sorts of disgusting garbage, they probably ran him off.

Soon after Mr. Gadget was saved from lethal injection, he was run over by a truck in front of his house on Highway 14. He ran into the woods and stayed hid out for three days before returning home with numerous cuts and gashes from head to tail, deep wounds that needed to be sewn up and his testicles swollen with one popped out of the scrotum. The vet wouldn't and couldn't sew him up because it had been too many days without treatment. He was sewn up, testicle removed, doctored and given antibiotics. He laid around the house for weeks on the brink of death. But (yes, "but") he survived and was back to his old self in a few months.

So, there he was, tongue hanging out and dragging the ground, one testicle, scars covering his nose , head and body. His new form of restraint was a plastic-coated, wire cable made for dogs. He was staked out in the yard with his new cable, minding his own business, dreaming of stinky garbage. Jason's brother, Cooter, shows up to mow the yard. Cooter makes a few rounds on his riding lawn mower, (you see where this is going?). As Cooter gets close to Mr. Gadget, he decides at the last minute to dart across Cooter's path. Cooter runs over the cable, and it wraps around the lawn mower blade. Cooter can't get the old worn-out mower to shut off and it's winding Mr. Gadget's cable around the shaft. Mr. Gadget's neck is being stretched as he has all four feet dug into the ground, kicking and squirming against the pull of the mower. Cooter is frantically trying to shut the mower off with no luck. The key broke off in the ignition, and he can't get it shut down. Slowly, Mr. Gadget is being drug into the twirling blades as he strains on his collar to try and escape certain death. Events unfolded in slow motion, like the old silent movies when the girl is tied to the train tracks and the train is getting closer! As Mr. Gadget is about to get sucked into the jaws of death, just inches away—the cable snaps! Mr. Gadget flees into the woods again to hide and calm his nerves.

Mr. Gadget returns home hours later. Cooter explained to Jason what had happened, and Jason got a new cable and staked out Mr. Gadget closer to the house. This should keep him safe and out of harm's way—right?

Jason lived in a trailer house (yes, a trailer house is what my country ass calls them—not a mobile home). Mr. Gadget is staked close to the front door of Jason's trailer house. He had about twenty or thirty feet of cable in which to run around in any direction.

A few days pass, and Jason comes home to find the metal skin of his front door ripped halfway off from the bottom up. There was blood all over the white door! Mr. Gadget is nowhere to be found, and then Jason notices Mr. Gadget's cable is trailing up the concrete steps and through the jagged metal hole that is now in his front door. Jason pried his door open and examines the outside metal that is smeared with blood and ripped loose from the frame. It looked like a bear or Big Foot had ripped into his house and injured itself on the sharp metal or had killed something!

To Jason's surprise, Mr. Gadget was lying in the floor, relaxing with a bleeding tongue and mouth. Evidently, he just wanted in the house, or maybe he was trying to get to the trash can and couldn't reach it…who knows? Jason screwed the metal skin back down on his front door and moved Mr. Gadget to a new location in the yard.

Jason has two sons, Adam and Blake. Adam and Blake found it quite amusing to wave the metal detector over Mr. Gadget's butt and listen to it "beep", indicating that it had located lead shot in his ass. I'll have to admit that I found it quite amusing myself. One morning after breakfast the boys attempted to feed Mr. Gadget some leftover pancakes with syrup and butter on them. Mr. Gadget sniffed, turned up his nose and dangling tongue and walked away.

"I can't believe that he won't eat pancakes," the boys said.

"Rub them in the dirt and give them to him!" Jason said.

So, the boys rubbed the pancakes in the dirt until they were disgusting looking and then made their offering to Mr. Gadget again. Mr. Gadget sniffed and eyeballed the nasty pancakes and then snatched them up and began to devour them!

"Look at that! That's crazy!" the boys exclaimed.

"I told you," Jason said. "If it's not disgusting, he won't eat it!"

Jason was doing some Spring cleaning and had a big fire outside in which he was burning limbs and discarded items. He cleaned out his frig and freezer and came across a package of out-of-date pork sausage. He figured that this was something Mr. Gadget would enjoy. Jason cut one end of the plastic wrapper open and offered it to Mr. Gadget. Mr. Gadget was not interested. I guess it wasn't rank enough. Jason shrugged and then tossed the package of sausage into the fire, plastic and all. The next morning, when he got up to check on the smoldering bonfire, he found Mr. Gadget digging and rooting like a hog in the ashes. Then like a treasure hunter, he paused and latched onto his prize and drug out the sausage package that had now become a black, crusty, burnt plastic and meat infused piece of disgusting grossness Then he began to chew and crunch on it like a pork rind or taco shell. Jason just shook his head and left Mr. Gadget standing in the ashes with his morning treat.

A pack of dogs came meandering through the countryside one day and spotted Mr. Gadget. I suppose they thought he was a weasel or an otter, I don't know. Anyway, they attacked him. Five or six big dogs had Mr. Gadget stretched out like a coon. Pulling him in all directions and biting him as he screamed and cried. Json heard his cries and came to the rescue, beating the dogs off of him and saving him from being ripped to pieces.

One day, Mr. Gadget went missing again. He had not returned home after dark or the next morning, Jason searched and called for Mr. Gadget all through the countryside.

After six or eight months, Jason conclude that Mr. Gadget must be dead, eaten by coyotes or maybe killed by other dogs. Knowing Mr. Gadget's nine lives or more, I told Jason that some kid or old woman probably started feeding his goofy looking self and kept him. I figured he's living indoors on someone's couch, eating cat food and watching soap operas. Who knows? He may show up again someday or in the newspapers.

BODY SHOP—-STRANGE DAYS

My first day at Carl Owens Truck and RV Collision Center was everything but normal. I rolled up into the parking lot in my '70 model Ford pickup. It was early 1990 something.

I stopped in the employee parking lot and directly in front of me, walking across the yard was a small, skinny, short fellow with short hair and horn rim glasses. He was headed South toward the truck shop. He was leaning in a forty-five-degree angle as if the wind were blowing ninety miles an hour. I thought, *"Damn! Wind's picked up a bunch!"* I step out of the truck, expecting a strong wind, but it's a calm day, overcast, but calm. I watched this individual speed walk to the truck shop at a forty-five-degree angle. I shook my head and headed to the manager's office.

Martin Crosby had hired me. Martin was a great guy, Vietnam Vet, Freemason, a sharp dresser and as "country" as I am. Also, assisting in managing and outside sales was Beauford. Beauford always had a big chew of tobacco in his jaw and a line of bullshit in his mouth. Beauford showed me around the shop. It's a big place covering 9 acres and containing five big shops. We walked past a cabover Peterbilt that was torn down to nothing but the floor and steering wheel. Its cab or what was left of it was kicked over at a forty-five-degree angle, exposing the engine. Climbing around on this skeleton of a truck like a monkey was Jason Kelley. Jason was popping rivets and assembling this truck like a wild man.

Beauford said, "If you want to know anything about this place or where anything is, ask that guy." He pointed at Jason and said, "He knows where everything is."

Jason needs a book of his own. He's that damn interesting and entertaining in my opinion. I unloaded my tool boxes with the help of an old fellow named, Neil. Neil was smoking a Pall Mall cigarette with no filter and was looking over the top of his glasses while driving a forklift. He pulled the forklift up to my tailgate and then drug one fork of the lift down the front of my shiny, red tool box. He didn't stop, slow down or say, *"I'm sorry"*. He just stuck the forks under my box and unloaded it.

His nephew, Kenny just shook his head and took a drag off his cigarette and said, "That's Uncle Neil. He's dangerous on that forklift."

Strange days were ahead. I just didn't know it. There were many strange and entertaining characters at this place.

Five days into my new job, I noticed everyone gathered at the front-end alignment pit. I walked up and asked, "What's up?" Everyone was looking toward the big window that opened into the manager's office.

They said, "We're watching Jason do his time for payroll."

Jason was seated in front of Beauford and Martin as they went down the list of repairs that he had completed for the week. We got paid on commission. Jason would sit calmly at first and then jump up on occasion and point out toward the shop or raise both hands in the air and wave them about in disagreement or dissatisfaction to the amount of time paid for each job.

Jason would jump up out of his chair and then sit down and review the next job with Beauford and Martin. It was like a silent movie. We couldn't hear what they were saying, but watched their lips moving and Jason pointing and slapping the desk while springing up and down every few minutes.

"What's wrong with him? I asked.

With a hillbilly twang, Kenny replied, " Well, he's upset about his time. He thinks they're getting to him on his hours."

Week after week, we gathered to watch the silent show. Jason pointed and jumped up and down and sometimes showed them his hands. Beauford and Martin sat and shook their heads and wrote down the hours for pay amid an array of shouts and hand waving. We ad-libbed what they said and enjoyed the show.

One day, after payroll was done, Jason came storming through the shop and dug around in his tool box until he found the biggest crescent wrench he had. He then walked over to the windshield rack, which was about twelve feet tall and had about ten or twelve windshields on it. Jason leapt as high as he could and sliced through about ten of the windshields with his crescent wrench like Thor with his hammer! Glass sprayed and scattered all around the glass rack.

Jason surveyed the damage and smiled. "That should be about the same money that they screwed me out of," he said.

I looked at Neil as he was cutting Bondo with the air file. He paused and pulled the no filter Pall Mall out of his mouth and shook his head. "That boy's a wild one!" he calmly said and then went back to work.

The next day, Beauford came scurrying through the shop with a customer. "I've got just what you need," he said as he led the guy toward the glass rack. He was talking and assuring the customer that he could help him out when he came to a skidding stop in front of the glass rack. Beauford almost swallowed his chew of tobacco as he gazed at the broken glass still on the floor and the vacant glass rack.

"What in the hell happened here?" he shouted and then looked over at me. I shrugged my shoulders and kept on fiberglassing a hood. He looked over at Neil. Neil just puffed his Pall Mall, shrugged and continued working.

"Well! I'll be damned! We did have what you needed, but I guess it broke!" Beauford said to the customer. Jason was giggling and glassing an R-model Mack hood.

The man in charge of the warehouse supplies was—-well, I'll call him "Garth". Garth weighed about four-hundred-fifty pounds. He had a small "Hitler" mustache and wore a baseball cap, chained smoked and sat on a stool all day. Yes, back in those days people smoked everywhere—-even in a warehouse full of paint and paint thinner. Garth also loaned money. Lots of guys there borrowed money from Garth and since he handed out the paychecks, he could keep tabs on his debtors. If you borrowed twenty dollars, next week you owed twenty-five dollars. If you borrowed one hundred dollars, the next week you owed one hundred and twenty-five dollars. Yes, Garth made more money, loaning money than he did working for Carl Owens.

Garth also began or ended each sentence with the word, "Sir". Garth proclaimed his love for Mr. Owens on a daily basis. "Oh, Sir, I love Mr. Owens. He's a wonderful man and allows me to work for him. If you threw me out of this place and into the street, I would crawl back in on my bloody hands and knees!" he would say. Garth would sing "Happy Birthday" over the P.A. system to anyone whose birthday it might be. It was awful!!

The little fellow that I witnessed walking at a forty-five-degree lean, owed Garth a few hundred dollars and hadn't paid. Garth went over to this house one night with intentions of collecting the debt. Garth beat on the door, yelled and cussed, but got no response from inside. Garth had come prepared. He unloaded several sheets of plywood and screwed them over each door and window of the small house and then left. Unbeknownst to Garth the forward leaning "welcher" was not home, He was out drinking up the money he owed to Garth, When he got home in an inebriated state, he was quite confused on how he could enter his house!

One day, a fellow employee insulted Garth. We'll call this employee "Kevin". Kevin was thin and frail-looking with a huge nose that made him look like a buzzard. Garth weighed about four hundred and fifty pounds and looked like a gorilla. Garth grabbed Kevin by the throat and lifted him with one hand and pressed him against the wall. All one hundred and twenty pounds of Kevin was off the floor, kicking and squirming while holding Garth's huge arm that was clamped around his buzzard-like neck. With his free hand, Garth was steadily puffing his cigarette and calmly talking to Kevin.

"Oh, Sir! You shouldn't talk to me like that, Sir!" Garth said. After a thorough choking, Kevin was released and left in a crumpled pile on the floor.

PARENTAL GUIDANCE for THIS STORY
STRANGE DAYS CONTINUE

Anytime someone thinks they have a work place story that can't be topped, I have an ace-in-the-hole that wins every time. If you think you've heard it all and nothing will surprise you, then I have a treat for you! I, myself used to think that I had heard it all and that there was nothing new under the sun, then this happened.

At this time, I am an estimator and assistant for the General Manager of Carl Owens Truck & RV Collision Center. The General Manager was Andy Wood. Andy had endured years of employees with various excuses for leaving work or not coming to work. Getting arrested at work or being in jail is average and the norm in our business...no big deal. I've been bailed out myself on Monday morning, but that's another story.

Body shop employees are somewhere on the scale between construction workers and prison inmates. At this moment, I've been thirty-five years in the business. I know what I'm talking about.

Andy's office and mine are connected by a doorway and we can easily hear and talk to each other which we do all day. Early, on Monday morning, I hear his phone being paged. The voice on the other end is one of our supervisors from the paint shop—-we'll call him "Frank".

"What do you need, Frank?" Andy asked.

"Pick up the phone," Frank said.

The rest of the conversation I'm listening to is just Andy talking and asking questions.

"What?"

"You broke what?"

"How'd you do that?"

"Are you sure it's broke?"

"It turned BLACK!?"

"NO! I DON'T want to see it!"

"Are you sure it's broke?"

"You looked it up on the internet?"

"How'd you break it?"

"You need to go to the doctor!"

"Yes! I believe you! No! I don't want to see it!"

"Bring me a doctor's excuse"

Andy slammed the phone down, put his head in his hands and said, "Ronald, you're not going to believe this!"

I stepped through the doorway to listen to the news, expecting to hear that Frank had broken his finger, hand, arm or something of that sort. We have forty employees and half of those are in the paint shop where Frank works. We repair trucks, trailers and other large equipment. There are times when people get hurt, handling large parts or equipment, especially when you're disassembling or reassembling things.

Andy is holding his head with both hands and shaking his head. "Ronald", (he used my full name instead of "Ron" so, I knew it was bad). "Ronald, Frank has broken his dick!" he calmly said.

I stared at him and said, "Bullshit!"

Andy nodded his head and said, "Yep! Broke his dick!"

"Up there in the paint shop—there's nothing but guys up there?" I asked.

"No, last night—he broke it last night!" Andy explained.

"Well, thank goodness it didn't happen at work," I said. "Workmen's Comp will never believe this shit!" I remarked. "Is he sure it's broke?"

"Yes!" Andy replied.

"How does he know it's broke? I asked.

"It turned BLACK! Andy replied.

At this point, Andy and I have started laughing. The rest of this conversation was me laughing until I was crying and holding my sides and Andy doing the same. It was some of the worst uncontrollable laughter that I've ever experienced.

Me – "It turned BLACK!?"

Andy – "Yep, he asked if I wanted to see it!"

Me – "Asked if you wanted to *see* it?"

Andy – "Yep! He didn't think that I would believe him if he didn't show it to me!"

Me – "I think you *should* look at it!"

Andy – "HELL, NO!"

Me – "So, he's sure it's broke?"

Andy – "Says he googled it, and he has all the symptoms."

The office is rattling with laughter, howls and tears,. It's all we can do to get these few words out. I'm glad a customer didn't come in as we couldn't have helped them if we had wanted to do so.

Me – "I would think you could know without googling if your dick was broke or not, especially if it turned black. I'm just glad he didn't break it in the paint shop."

Andy – "I can't believe this crap!"

Me – "Oh, this is great. I have never, never, ever, ever heard anything like this, and I've heard a lot!"

We regained our composure, somewhat and carried on our daily chores with occasional outbursts of laughter, of course.

This type of entertaining information is hard to keep to yourself and by midday the whole shop was abuzz with the news of Frank and his broke dick.

Around lunch time, Andy was at his desk and I and several of the guys had gathered in the adjoining break room. Frank pulls up in front of the office and slowly and carefully walks in carrying a doctor's excuse.

"Here's my doctor's excuse," Frank said as he held the paper out to Andy.

"Give that to Ron and he'll make a copy," Andy said.

I was trying not to smile or laugh as I took the note from him. I made a copy as Frank walked stiff legged around the office, talking to Andy. The copy machine was in the break room where the flock of body techs were eating lunch and snickering. Frank entered the break room to retrieve his copy of the doctor's excuse. As I handed it to him, I asked "Are you going to be OK, Frank?" I was seriously concerned at this point.

"Yeah, the doctor told me to go home and keep it elevated," Frank said.

And then this just popped into my brain and exited through my mouth, "Isn't that how you broke it in the first place?"

The break room exploded with howls and laughter. We were all laughing and crying again, except for Frank.

Frank snatched the note out of my hand and with a scowl on his face, in a pissed off tone said, "If you ever break your dick, I'm going to laugh at you!"

As Frank slowly and carefully turned to limp away, I told him, "Frank, if I ever do break my dick, you will never know it! I will show up with a cast on my leg or on crutches or a neck brace, but I will not let anyone know that I broke my dick. I will fake some other injury as a reason why I can't walk or why I went to the doctor.

Frank just looked over his shoulder and said, "All you sons-a-bitches, I'm going to laugh at you if you break your dicks!"

That just caused more laughter. Frank was off work for a few days and then returned to an array of ribbing and jokes, They changed his name for a little while and started calling him "B.D.". He wasn't shy about talking about it and giving information when asked how he was feeling.

"The doctor says it might be crooked or have a knot on it from now on. We'll have to wait and see!" he would say.

I never saw it and don't want to see it, but he says it healed up. I don't know. If you can top that as work place related story, please let me know.

No Shit…True Story!

ONE BOAT PARADE

My buddy, Dennis Stewart and his friend, O.L. Guy were exiting either Cox Restaurant or Fuller's in Tyler, Texas. They were climbing into their truck when coming down the street in front of them was a black man driving an old Dodge pickup, towing a boat. Midship of this boat was another black man, seated in the driver's seat of the boat. He was holding the steering wheel of the boat while smiling and waving at people on both sides of the street as he passed by them as if he were in a parade.

"Would you look at that!?" O.L. said as he put a chew of tobacco in his jaw and then spit.

"Isn't that something!?" Dennis said as they watched the one boat parade go by at a pretty fast pace. They also witnessed the pickup bounce across the railroad track crossing or was it a man hole cover, pot hole or something of that nature which caused the boat in tow to come unlatched and separate from the truck. At this point, the boat driver has placed both hands on the steering wheel and is spinning left and right in an attempt to correct the problem, but to no avail. The boat gains speed and passes his would-be tow vehicle which has begun to apply the brakes. The boat's captain has become wide-eyed and frantic as he is trying to steer the runaway boat. Waving to the masses is no longer a priority.

The boat then picked up speed and passed the tow vehicle which is safely stopped on the side of the street. It had to be an exciting ride as the nose of the boat dipped forward, and the trailer tongue began to spark and skid on the pavement right up until it impacted a green trash dumpster at a fast click. Upon impact, the boat's captain was catapulted out of the boat, over the dumpster and onto some parked cars, spread-eagle.

Right about then is when O.L. swallowed his chew of tobacco and started puking in the floor board. Dennis was laughing uncontrollably and trying to get out of the truck. Other people were rushing to check on the boat's captain. I'm not sure about the end results or injuries, but I do have some advice…

…SAFETY CHAINS, PEOPLE!…SAFETY CHAINS!!!

KALASHNIKOV-AK47

It's always useful to speak more than one language. I speak English, Redneck, Hillbilly, Bodyshop, Biker, Truck Driver, Farmer, Cowboy and a very little bit of Spanish or as we call it in Texas-Mexican. Then one day it happened! I was able to speak Russian and with very little effort had gained some Russian friends.

It was kind of an accident when I discovered that I speak Russian! One day a couple of Russian Gypsy, truck part buyers came by the shop wanting to purchase some of our discarded truck parts. They spoke pretty good English with a heavy Russian accent. These two squared-headed, cigarette-smoking young men seem to be hard workers. We didn't have any parts that fit their buying criteria, but we conversed for a few minutes and discovered that they were from Bulgaria. I told them that my favorite AK47, which I owned, was made in Bulgaria.

"I love those Bulgarian AK47s," I told them.

Their faces lit up as if I were an old friend, and they slapped my back and shook my hand. I thought they were going to hug me. They once again went over the list of parts they needed to buy and offered to pay more for them if I had any, just because I knew where Bulgaria was and had good things to say about it.

The next such occasion arose at a furniture store in Tyler, Texas. My wife, Karen and I were picking up some things for our cabin in Oklahoma. The young man helping us had a slight Russian accent. We'll call him "Ivan", (this is probably Slavic, but...Oh, well!). As Ivan began to check-out and add-up our purchases, I asked him where he was from. "Bullard", he responded (meaning Bullard, Texas).

"No, not where you live now. Where are you originally from?" I asked him. "You sound like maybe you are from Russia," I replied nicely.

He looked around cautiously and responded, "Yes, Russia," and continued to punch buttons on his computer.

"You, Russians sure know how to make good vodka and great weapons," I told him. "I love the AK47. I have several," I added.

"You like the Kalashnikov?" he asked.

No, I *love* the Kalashnikov! I exclaimed.

He stopped what he was doing and asked, "Have you ever shot a fully automatic Kalashnikov?"

"No, I haven't," I replied.

Once again, he looked around cautiously and then leaned over the counter toward me and in a low voice said, "When I was in the 'program', I got to shoot and carry a Kalashnikov." Then he smiled.

"OK! I'm listening. Tell me more," I said.

"Well, in the 'program' you only have fully automatic Kalashnikovs, so they teach you to pull the trigger and count to three and then release it so that you don't waste ammo. But me, I'm a slow counter and by the time I would count to three, the gun is pointing up in the air from the force of the repercussion. So, they yell at me, and I have to learn to count faster," he said in his Russian accent.

"That's interesting. I like that," I told him.

He smiled and started punching buttons again to complete our purchase.

"I'm going to give you an extra five percent off your purchase because you like Russian Kalashnikov," he said.

Now *I* was smiling, and Karen was shaking her head in amazement.

He then asked for my last name, and I answered, "Armstrong", same as the astronaut…Uncle Neil" I added.

Ivan paused again and looked at me like I was a rock star. Let me tell you something people, one thing that Russians know and love is anything Space-related or Space History. They don't care if it's Russian or American.

"Neil Armstrong is your Uncle?! he asked with great enthusiasm.

"Well, all of us Armstrongs are kin somehow. We all came from Scotland," I replied.

Ivan turned back to his computer and said, " I give you another ten percent off because Neil is your Uncle!"

"Wow! Thanks Ivan. You are an alright dude!" I told him as Karen continued to shake her head and roll her eyes.

Since he was in a generous mood, I asked him about a large, framed print of some black bears that he had. I thought it was probably more expensive than I cared to pay. Ivan slashed the price to the point that I had to buy it. It now hangs directly over the front door on the inside of our cabin in Oklahoma.

It turned out that Ivan was also the manager of the store and as we finished up with our purchases, Ivan confided something else to me. "When I was in the 'program', I got to meet Kalashnikov, himself,," he said.

"That is very cool, Ivan. I love stories like that," I told him.

The third time that I was able to use my Russian language skills was when a Russian truck driver stopped by with mechanical problems. He spoke almost no English. "Fix truck," he said. That was the best he could do besides pointing to show me the problem as he rambled in Russian.

"Come with me to my office," I told him as I motioned for him to follow me. I held up one finger and pointed to the telephone. "Give me one minute and I'll call someone to help you," I told him.

He had a confused look on his face and nodded "yes". I made a couple of calls to some mechanic shops that could help him and told them the situation. As I was making calls, this Russian dude, we will call him "Igor", was examining my bullet collection on the wall and all of the bullets, knives and military paraphernalia that I have on my desk. Then he spotted the guns I have on the counter behind my desk and the AK47 leaned up in the corner behind my desk. When I hung up the phone, he was bent over, looking at my rifles with his face about a foot away from the weapons.

"You like those?" I asked.

He looked at me and with a serious look on his face, jabbered something in Russian.

"I love those Kalashnikov rifles," I told him as I pointed at my AK47. He put his hand on my shoulder and said, "You know Kalashnikov?"

Yes, I know Kalashnikov," I said.

He put both hands on his chest and said, "I know Kalashnikov."

He put his hands on my shoulders and asked, "You say, you love Kalashnikov?"

"YES!" I answered.

"I love Kalashnikov!" he said and then pointed at the AK47, indicating he wanted to hold it.

"Go ahead, pick it up and look at it," I told him

When Igor picked up this gun, he transformed into someone else. He grabbed the gun and held it like a woman holds a baby with gentle, loving hands and a look of pure joy on his face. Then he stood at attention, shouldered the rifle and began to march around my office as if he were possessed. He was speaking Russian as he stood at attention, did an about face, a march and several gun tricks which included spinning my AK47 around, beside and in front of him. He put on an amazing show of military-style skill and disciplines that ended with him standing at attention in front of me with the AK47 at his side. He gently returned the rifle to its place in the corner. He then turned and showed me his belt buckle as he continued to jabber in Russian. It was some type of Russian military buckle and evidently this gun had just brought back some good memories for Igor. For the next forty minutes, I listened as Igor talked and showed me pictures of his truck, home in Florida, dog, wife and cars. His wife didn't look too bad in that bikini on the beach—-just sayin'. At the end of our one-sided conversation, Igor hugged me and walked to the door to exit, he then turned and saluted me as he stiffened his body to stand as straight and tall as possible. He left, and I've never seen him again.

So, folks, let this be a lesson. Guns can be an international language of love. It's not always about the destruction they can do. Guns are like a car, a piano or anything people enjoy and are passionate about. They *can* bring back good memories.

Remember, folks all you need to survive in this life is Jesus and a .45 but keep that AK47 within reach!

M/C LIFE

I have loved motorcycles since I saw the movie C.C. & Company, starring Joe Namath. I was about five years old. I saved up my money, and when I was about eleven years old, I bought my first dirt bike. After this, it was my first street bike when I was sixteen and after that a few Harleys.

There is nothing like the feeling of riding. It's not for everyone, but when it's your thing—-you know it! If you haven't experienced it, then I can't explain it, but if you have, then you know exactly what I mean. The world is different on the back of a bike. I grew up riding horses, maybe that's why I like a motorcycle. It's a similar feeling, just faster and no bucking or brushing.

The only thing better than riding is riding with some solid Brothers around you; a patch on your back, knees in the breeze, a brother beside you, in front and behind you, going eighty miles an hour, making every move or lane change that your Brothers make. There's no other feeling like it.

There is a difference in M/C life and biker life. An M/C (Motorcycle Club) has officers who rule and govern in the best interests and actions of the club and its members. It also has a code of ethics and rules. You answer to your Brothers and Officers for disorderly behavior, or you may seek their help and assistance if you need help with anything or anyone.

A biker rides and enjoys doing "biker things" but answers to no one but himself. There's nothing wrong with that…it's all good. But (yes, there's that "but" again) the M/C world is a subculture that only a few people get to walk amongst. Most outside that culture do not know or understand the rules and protocol that we live by and respect.

I have five solid Brothers that I love and respect. We don't want anything from each other. We enjoy spending time together, whether it's riding, working or just hanging out. Cracker, Big Daddy, PeeWee, T-Bird, Rain Man, all these Brothers mean the world to me. They also keep me entertained.

Brother T-Bird keeps me entertained by unintentionally revealing details about his everyday life that probably shouldn't be shared or pointing out obvious things that we waste no time commenting on. Brother PeeWee is a wealth of political knowledge, Local, State and Federal. I really know that I'm in for a treat when the story starts out, "when I was in prison".

Big Daddy with his deep voice is always direct and to the point when making his short but accurate comments on any "off the wall" subjects or side stories that T-Bird or PeeWee come up with.

Cracker is always meticulous and well-thought out on any subject and quick to jump at any chance (normally) to berate any of us who have said something that would leave us wide open for insult or sport.

Rain Man likes things orderly and done correctly and timely. He's always early for events. Anything from his bike to any other project he's involved in has to be perfect or he's not happy. He listens and watches in amazement sometimes to the array of conversations and comments that "go South" in any given meeting or bullshit session we have.

I, myself (Hillbilly) like things to be as orderly as possible, but revel in the opportunity to listen to any dysfunctional conversation that we veer into. I usually do not have opportunity to comment because of side-splitting pain and near hyperventilation from laughing at and with my Brothers. They say

I have a contagious laugh that sounds something like the cartoon dog, Muttley. They *almost* forced me to change my name!

Regardless of how much good we do for different causes, whether it be for needy children, the homeless, elderly, veterans or any of the many, many charities we support, sponsor and donate to, we as M/C members are looked at with disdain and suspicion by most law enforcement officers or LEOs. There are a few that view us and judge us as individuals and for the good we do for society, but they are few, mostly those who know us on a personal level. That being said, it leads me into this story.

For two or three months out of the year, we attend city council meetings across East Texas to bring awareness to motorcycles and motorcycle safety awareness.

T-Bird, me and Southern Reepers Blinker were in Kilgore at one such meeting. There were about thirty LEOs at this meeting, ten in front of us and about ten or twelve to both sides of us. Yes, as bikers, we looked a little out of place or suspect in a room full of LEOs and firemen dressed in their uniforms. As the room continued to fill up, T-Bird made an observation aloud, "We're surrounded by cops!" At which each and every cop in front of and beside us turned and stared at us. I just smiled and put my arm around T-Bird and addressed the mob of unfriendly stares, "Y'all just have to excuse my Brother. He gets a little excited sometimes." They turned their attention away from us and T-Bird began to explain aloud, "I didn't mean anything by it. It just seems strange having all these cops around us." All the cops took another glance at us, and I just smiled. "I understand T-Bird, you don't' have to explain," I told him.

The Police Chief had seated himself directly in front of me, and when the city council got around to our proclamation T-Bird tapped him on the shoulder and asked if he would take our picture with the city council members. The Chief was very friendly and said, "Certainly!" T-Bird handed him his phone. About the time the Chief got his hands on the phone, a message popped up on our M/C thread. T-Bird exclaimed, "Oh! Don't read that!" and he reached and grabbed his phone from the clutches of the law. The Chief had a surprised and puzzled look on his face. T-Bird cleared the message and handed his phone back to the Chief.

"If any messages pop up, don't read them," he said.

"The Chief just smiled and said, "I probably get worse messages than whatever that was."

I don't think he understood the relevance of having access to our M/C thread. Not that we discuss anything bad or illegal. It's just the irony of willingly handing "The Man" your phone. As a matter of fact, the last message of our thread at that very minute was from me. It read, *"I hope I can get T-Bird out of here before we get arrested. There are at least thirty cops here."*

We did our deal and got pictures with the city council and then exited the building. The look on Blinker's face was priceless when T-Bird made his loud observation about our current situation, and he was as relieved as I was to leave that meeting.

In our previous life, we hosted three-day events, a run or a rally, whatever you want to call it. At these bike rallies, that last three days there is always someone who wants to be disorderly.

One such individual, who was about six foot, five inches, tall and weighed at least two hundred eighty pounds and was made of solid muscle, decided he wanted to be a problem. For a day and a half, he had not said two words and was a model citizen. Now, at one a.m. on Sunday morning, he decides he wants to cause problems and start a fight. About eight of my Brothers and me were circling him trying to talk him down and diffuse the situation. He continued to be belligerent and adamant about wanting to fight.

"I'll kick all y'all's asses!" he shouted with fists clinched and shoulders bowed and bulging like a bull's.

I am standing directly in front of the guy, talking to him, trying to hold his attention in case three or four of my Brothers want to grab him and escort him back to his camp. But (yes, "but") out of my right eye's peripheral vision, I see PeeWee running toward us at a fast clip. When within eight feet of the raging individual PeeWee jumps up in the air like he's doing a slam dunk and comes down with a fist crashing into the guy's left ear! This dude is more than twice as big as Pee Wee but with one punch Pee Wee has him on the ground and on top of him just wearing the dude out with lefts and rights to the head!

We all just stand there for a few seconds in amazement, thinking that PeeWee would back off. But (yes, "but"), I guess it was feeling good to him and he wasn't stopping. About four of us pulled PeeWee off, and four other Brothers picked up the big dude. The disorderly individual had become docile and calm as his eyes spun around in different directions with blood dripping out of his left ear which had swollen to look like a huge cauliflower and blood poured from his squashed nose! He gracefully and cooperatively let two Brothers assist him to his tent. His posture was somewhere between a wet dishrag and a slinky.

"You boys were talking too much and making no headway. Sometimes you just gotta take action," Peewee said.

BROTHER CRACKER QUOTES

"Being president of an M/C is much like herding cats—wild cats."

Brother Big Daddy is a tall dude with a long ponytail, long beard and a deep voice. He lives up to his name. On one of our fourth of July campouts at Lake Hawkins. Big Daddy had a misadventure that we would not have known about had he not told this on himself. I'll set the scene:

We had campers and tents parked in a semi-circle at the non-electric, no hook-ups section of camping at Lake Hawkins. It being hot weather and a holiday, we all had some adult beverages, and some had more adult beverages than others. Some time during the night's festivities, Big Daddy saw the need to ease off into the woods, away from all the noise. He decided to take a short nap and then rejoin the fun later. He may or may not have had more beers than he thought. Upon awakening from his nap, he noticed that the night had given way to the light of dawn. He stood up, rubbed the sleep from his eyes and gazed off into the forest in front of him.

"Well, F_ _k! Where the hell am I?" he asked himself. He looked a little to the right and to the left, he stood and listened. He couldn't hear anything except the birds singing.

"Well, f_ _ k! I guess I'm lost in the f_ _king woods!" he cursed. "I don't know where the f_ _ k I'm at!" he declared. It looked like a hopeless situation.

"I wander off into the woods for some peace and quiet and this is what I get?!" he thought. He stood there with his hands on his hips pondering which direction to go. Disgusted with the situation, he turns around to look for a good trail and directly behind him about a hundred yards is camp. No shit! Ask him about it!

Brother Rain Man is a great Road Captain, make no mistake about it. But his eating habits and mine are a little different. He says that sometimes he gets busy and forgets to eat! My days are *planned* around when I eat!

On one particular run we made from Tyler, Texas to Hot Springs, Arkansas, Rain Man attempted to starve me to death! He didn't do this intentionally, of course. We had been on the road since around 8 a.m. and had stopped at a convenience store for fuel. I was inclined to grab a snack or a sausage and biscuit, corn dog or something of substance since I really have a need to eat about every two hours if at all possible.

"No, don't get anything to eat," Rain Man said. "I'm going to take you to a Steak & Shake. You'll like it," he adds.

"OK, sounds good," I reply

So, here we go. I'm riding along with my Brothers, enjoying the wind and freedom of the road. I'm thinking about some food as I ride and listen to my music. Thirty minutes pass, and I start looking for a Steak & Shake! An hour passes, and I'm looking at every sign I see, hoping it says, "Steak & Shake". A few hours pass, and I'm dying, my stomach thinks my throat's been cut! Almost out of fuel and so hungry I could eat the bottom rocker on T-Bird's cut, we pull into a gas station.

Rain Man pulls off his helmet and says, "I don't know what happened to that "Steak & Shake". I guess they closed it or changed the name."

"Brother, I don't care where or what we eat. I'm way past needing food, I'm feeling poorly," I tell him.

"Well, we're almost to Hot Springs. We will find something soon," he said.

"Cool, let's go! I'm freaking starving!" I reply.

So, here we go again headed toward Hot Springs. My stomach is killing me, and I'm about to die! Rain Man slows down and makes a left-hand turn signal. We pull into a liquor store! OMG! I'm about to die, and these freaks go to the liquor store! I love my Brothers and Sisters but when I'm hungry, I get kinda' "pissy!" I begrudgingly pull into the liquor store and kill my bike, pull off my helmet and say, "WTF?"

Rain Man is grinning and says, "We gotta' get some beer and Julie wants a bottle of Jim Beam"

My Brothers know how I am about food, and they found this slightly amusing with the exception that some of them were getting hungry too! Within a few miles of the liquor store, we found a catfish restaurant, and my disposition turned back into my usual ray of sunshine (if you disagree—-write your own book).

I swore that I would never let Rain Man forget about the time he nearly killed me with a lack of food, so here it is in black and white.

Love you, Brother!

CRACKER QUOTES

"This pickle beer pairs nicely with pizza!" Ya just had to be there.

I have more stories about the M/C life, but I'm considering a book about that all by itself. And I'm sure more quotes from Cracker will surface at some point also.

BIG FOOT AT LAKE PALESTINE

Some of you will know this dude. His name is Robert Booth. Rob is tatted from his neck to his knuckles and a fun guy to be around. But (yes…"but"), Rob got serious when he told me about his experience that he had in a secluded part of Lake Palestine while fishing from a flat bottom boat with two paddles. Rob and two of his buddies had permission to gain access to Lake Palestine via a friend's private property. They had the combination to the gate padlock, unloaded the boat and paddled deep into the back side of the lake. He stated the fish were biting great as they were casting toward the heavily wooded shoreline. They were facing the woods with their backs toward open water, when all of the sudden a huge rock or boulder hits the water directly behind them. KERPLUNK! It startled them, and Rob noticed something tall and hairy walking through the trees in front of them. He got a good look at it.

"There's no mistake what we saw. It was a Big Foot! It was tall and hairy. I got a good look at it as it walked through the trees going away from us. This is a secluded, hard to get to place!" Rob said.

They reeled in their lines and began to paddle fast and hard to get back to their truck. "We were scared to death!" Rob said.

Before Rob started telling me this story, he had walked up to me at a party and put both hands on my shoulders, looked me in the eye and said, "I've got to talk to you about Big Foot." This is as serious as I have ever seen Rob. He never smiled while telling me this and was so adamant that it caused me to believe him even though the friend that was with him at that moment was laughing at him.

He continued his story with hand gestures and urgency in his voice. "We paddled like hell to get back to the truck. We threw all our shit in the back and jumped in at the same time. We were scared to death! When we jumped in and locked the doors we realized we were all in the back seat! It's starting to get dark, and no one wants to get out to get in the driver's seat! Then after that gets settled, we crank up and start trying to get the hell out of there. When we get to the gate, we realize someone has to get out and unlock the gate. It's dark by now. No one wants to get out of the truck, We're three grown ass men—not scared of anything, but now we're terrified! So, we do 'Rock, Paper, Scissors' to see who will open the gate . This thing is real. I saw it!" Rob said.

BIG FEETS ON KICKAPOO CREEK

My friend, Shane told me of an experience that he had when he was about eight years old while with his Uncle Timmy on a fishing trip on Kickapoo Creek.

With Uncle Timmy in the lead, they hiked deep into the words, following Kickapoo Creek. As Shane put it, "Uncle Timmy was kinda' different. Uncle

Timmy was a bit unusual, but a good fisherman. The fish were biting, and they were catching them left and right. Just about sundown a huge splash came from the right of them as something big was thrown into the water.

"What was that?" Shane asked.

Uncle Timmy was now building a campfire. He had no intention of leaving his fishing spot now that the fish had started biting good. "Those are them Big Feets, throwing things in the water. They trying to scare us off. But we're not leaving," Uncle Timmy said as he added sticks to the fire until it was burning high and bright.

Shane said that just outside the light of the fire in the shadows of the trees and brush something was stomping around and breaking limbs, making grunting noises and still throwing things.

"That's just them Big Feets. They won't hurt you. They don't like the fire," Uncle Timmy told Shane.

Shane said that they caught a lot of fish but never got a good look at the Big Feets who harassed them.

HOSS & THE SPIRITS

I have a Masonic Brother who also rides with an M/C. We will call him, "Hoss". Hoss retired from the Terrell State Hospital. It' a public psychiatric hospital built around the year 1885.

Hoss declares that there are a lot of old spirits that still reside in the State Hospital, whether it's spirits of the dead or just spirits of another world, he's unsure of. Maybe some of both. Some patients would be brought in with shackles around their feet.

"You can't walk when you're shackled, you have to kinda' shuffle," Hoss says. "When you get eight or ten people shackled and shuffling down the hallway, it makes an eerie and distinct sound. You know what's coming down the hall toward you, but you never know what to expect," he said.

The mentally insane and demonic possession date back to Biblical times, and who knows what accompanies these poor, tormented souls to this hospital.

The oldest section of the hospital was no longer in use and was a separate building from where Hoss worked. There was no phone service or utilities in this building, yet they still received calls from the building on a weekly basis. They would cautiously answer the call that indicated that it was coming from the abandoned non-functioning building.

There was never a response from the other end of the line. Was it a call for help that couldn't be heard in this world or just a lonely spirit that wanted to hear a human voice or perhaps it was an attempt to aggravate or annoy the staff.

After years of these ghostly phone calls from unworking and abandoned phone systems, a security guard asked Hoss if he wanted to accompany him to check out the old building and determine where the calls were coming from. Hoss is a great big fellow who also lives up to his name. Maybe the guard felt safe with someone of Hoss's stature. They entered the old building slowly looking around from room-to-room, rechecking the phones, still no service. After a close inspection and finding nothing and no one and no phone service, Hoss and the guard returned to their nightly duties. After this the phone calls stopped. Maybe the spirit just needed to be acknowledged or maybe it gave up on being heard or seen and conceded its fate.

Hoss also confided in me that one time when they had restrained a violent patient to their bed and the patient was placed in an observation room, the bed began to bounce at least six inches off the floor and bounced all the way around the room. This patient proclaimed to be possessed by a demon. I feel certain that they were. We will gather more stories from Hoss about the State Hospital.

COCAINE & CHURCH

Our M/C, DESMADRES M/C plays host to the Iron Horse Biker Church every Sunday. One or more of us unlocks the clubhouse at 10 a.m. every Sunday to allow the preacher and audio-video personnel to prepare for services. The preacher, his wife and all of those involved in his ministry are a part of the Biker Community. They provide outreach programs to the homeless and needy as well as being active in motorcycle awareness, safety and biker's rights.

As a club, we give to a wide variety of charities and help those in need as well as supporting the church in any way needed including providing a place to worship.

We are used to being profiled and considered suspect looking just because we dress differently, look different, ride a Harley and wear a M/C patch on our backs. But we don't expect to be profiled by our own people.

I opened up the clubhouse for church one Sunday around 10 a.m. I took a seat behind the bar and poured a cup of coffee. There are people from various clubs that attend this church. We ride our bikes; we wear our cuts and pray and worship just like the "suit and tie" church crowds do. The preacher's wife was walking by the pool table and on top of the table beside the pool sticks was a zip lock bag with chalk dust in it for chalking your hands while shooting pool. She picked up the zip lock bag with the small amount of chalk dust in it, held it out in front of her and brought it to me, and with a whisper she says, "I think someone left this laying out." As I took the bag of high grade, uncut chalk dust from her, I said with a whisper, "It's chalk dust for the pool table," and handed it back. She took the bag from me with an embarrassed look on her face and said, "Oooohh, ok." She then turned and returned the chalk bag, hanging it on the peg above where she found it.

Desparadoes, Throwed Off was sitting at the bar, found this quite entertaining. All my Brothers got a good laugh when I told them about this. Yes, we're a three-piece patch M/C. No, we don't sell drugs, run guns or deal in human trafficking. We will get behind a good charity and help anyone we can and Yes! we have some of the best chalk dust you can find for shooting pool and it's FREE!

THE PASSWORD

A Brother Mason told me this story about his Uncle. Some of you know who told me this. It was the turn of the century, the early 1900's and horses were still the main mode of transportation. My Uncle was a horse trader and traveled all over Texas buying and selling horses. He was also a Mason, so whenever he was in a new town he would locate the Masonic Lodge building and at night he would check and see if there were any lights on inside. This would indicate a meeting night, and he would knock on the door and introduce himself and also prove himself to be a Mason through certain handshakes, signs or words known only to other Masons. This would entitle him to partake in the meeting or ceremony that was taking place not to mention some conversation and possibly a meal.

On one such occasion, he had located the Masonic Lodge building in this small Texas town and later that night he noticed some lights on inside. It was late but he was in need of some Brotherly conversation, so he headed toward the Lodge building and around to the back door. Most Lodges were two-story buildings in those days, the lower part was usually a school, Post Office or Church.

Uncle knocked on the door and waited. In a few seconds, he heard from inside, "What's the password?" Then the door swung open and there stood a white-robed, hooded Klansman holding a lantern. It startled Uncle and he jumped backwards, exclaiming, "I'll be a son-of-a-bitch!"

The big Klansman stood aside and held his lantern toward the staircase that led to the second story and said, "Come in, worthy Brother!"

A HAUNTING AND A .45

Another Brother told this about his Uncle. This story came from somewhere between Red Springs and Lindale, Texas.

Sometime during the first half of the 1900's, my Uncle had taken part in a lynching, A bad man who needed to be dealt with had committed a heinous crime and paid for it at the end of a rope.

Even when right is on your side, the taking of a life weighs heavy on a man's mind and can spark all kinds of thoughts and distractions. It was early to mid-1900's and Uncle was walking back home up a path and across a pasture, carrying a lantern. He was almost home and had crawled through a barbed wire fence. When he got through the fence, he stood up and there is the man he had just lynched standing only inches from his face! With lightening reflexes, he draws his .45 and shoots the guy twice, and the guy falls to the ground! Uncle picks up his lantern that he had sat on the ground while crawling through the fence and raises it over the body. Uncle said, "I had just killed the best damn milk cow there ever was!"

THE ROTTWEILER AND THE EMU

I was out in my front yard on Highway 14, five miles North of Hawkins, Texas, when I heard hounds baying and dogs barking. It sounded as if they were headed in my direction. As I looked up, I could see coming toward me at a high rate of speed a large emu. Yes! An emu! You know, the big birds that are almost as big as an ostrich. This dude was picking 'em up and putting 'em down! He looked like the Road Runner on the cartoons and not far behind the emu was a pack of dogs barking, baying, howling and having a fit. They were hot on his trail! I'm sure these dogs had never seen one of these critters before. I hadn't seen too many of them myself much less one running down Highway 14. Before it reached me it took a hard right and zipped down the blacktop road in front of my house. The emu seemed to know where he was going. The dogs did a boot leg turn and continued their pursuit of the leggy monster.

I stood there watching. I thought, *"Damn! I've seen some strange shit, but this just hit the top ten of the list."* The show was just getting started, it's just that I didn't know it. I listened as the barking and baying faded down County Road 3800 until I couldn't hear them anymore. I continued with my morning chores in the front yard, thinking that I would never see that again. In about thirty minutes, I look up and here comes this damn emu from across the road, heading straight toward me, across Highway 14 and through the ditch into my yard! I had a leaf rake in my hand and was prepared to defend myself against the feathered monster. Emus evidently have poor eyesight because when it was within ten feet of me, it put on the brakes and skidded to a stop as it back peddled and spun around to streak across my neighbor's yard. Heading back South now, this hot mess of a giant bird passed within five feet of my neighbor's Rottweiler which was chained to one of his two, front porch posts. The dog watched with curiosity and twitched his head from side-to-side as the big bird approached him at high speed. Then as the bird zipped past him—-WHOOSH!—-the dog went ape shit crazy! Growling, barking and hitting the end of his chain! On his second lunge, the front porch post which was about twelve inches by twelve inches square gave way and broke loose from its anchors in the concrete and the roof! Here goes the Rottweiler dragging a big chain attached to a ten foot, twelve by twelve post! It wasn't slowing him down. He was a big dog and all four feet were digging and kicking up dirt. I don't know what happened to the first pack of dogs. I never saw them again. But now the emu was being pursued by a large, shackled Rottweiler.

I stood there shaking my head and once again thought, *"I've never seen anything like this!"* But (yes…"but"), it wasn't over. I watched the ensuing chase until both bird and dog faded from my view. Later that afternoon, my neighbor returned home and was inspecting his porch where a post and a dog were missing. I walked over and told him about the day's events. He searched for his dog, but only found his porch post about a mile down the road. It was scraped and skinned but still useable. Late that evening, his dog returned home, crawling on his belly and refusing to stand up. He had a huge knot protruding from his head and gashes on his body. After two or three weeks, the Rotti healed up, but still preferred to crawl on his belly most of the time, and it never barked again.

"That damn emu ruined my dog!" my neighbor complained.

Hey Folks, stay the hell away from emus. They're dangerous!

BORDER CROSSING

My Mexican buddy, Raphael is a hard-working, good guy and has made me laugh a lot. He told me that he swam across the Rio Grande three times. The first time it was with his cousin, who was a lifeguard. He told Ralph to take off his clothes and let him take them across for him. Since his cousin was a much better swimmer and the clothes would only weigh him down, Ralph agreed. Ralph's cousin made it across the Rio Grande to the other side and motioned for Ralph to come across. It had been raining a lot and the Rio Grande had swollen and was running hard and fast. Ralph told me that about halfway across, the current started to carry him away and then it swept him downriver like a feather in a flood. He almost drowned, but struggled until he made it to the Texas side. Now, he was on the riverbank, naked! He tried to make his way back upriver. He was hiding behind every small bush and tree he could find until he finally found his cousin and retrieved his clothes.

Another time, Ralph told me about a guy who was hiding in the trunk of a car while crossing the border. He had been in there for some time and when his amigos crossed into Texas, the Border Patrol pulled them aside and asked a few questions. Then, they looked the car over and one of the officers knocked on the trunk of the car. KNOCK, KNOCK, KNOCK. From inside the trunk the guy asked, "Can I get out now?"

"You certainly can," the officer replied.

Raphael says that two other guy's saved their money for a long time to be able to come to Texas and make a new start. The day came for them to leave their homes in Mexico City, and they hopped on a train and hid in a box car. They rode the train for several days, eating and drinking provisions which they had brought with them. After three or four days, the train stops at a large train yard and the duo jumps out. They start making their way through the trainyard, hiding behind and between box cars. A man sees them and yells at them, "What are you guys doing?"

They answer, "We're hiding from the immigration police !"

The man answers back " There is NO immigration police in Mexico !"

These guys had ridden a train for three or four days in the wrong direction! The had gone South, deeper into Mexico. It took all of the money they had saved to get back to their homes.

A TASTE OF TEXAS

Ralph said that when they were finally able to catch the right train going to Texas, they ran out of food and water before they got to where they wanted to be, The train made a stop and they could see a store on the other side of the highway. They jumped off the train and ran as fast as they could to the store, went in and grabbed four cans of Wolf Brand Chili and some drinks, then hurried back to the box car before the train took off again.

"You know, I couldn't read or speak English back then and Wolf Brand Chili has a picture of a wolf on it. Alpo dog food has a picture of a German Shepherd on it. I'm pretty sure that I ate dog food that day!" he said.

Ralph worked for a construction company and for six months straight, he ate lunch at a Sonic restaurant across the street from the job site. He couldn't speak English very well, so he asked some of his fellow workers how to order at the Sonic. "The only English I knew for six months was 'double meat cheese burger with extra jalapenos'!" he said. "That's the only food that I knew how to order in English,. I *hate* jalapenos! I just didn't know how to tell them *not* to put them on the burger. My co-workers thought it was funny," he said.

LET SLEEPING DOGS LIE!

Ole' Ralph has a big heart and will help anyone or anything. He was on his way home one, hot Summer day and noticed two dogs laying in the middle of a yard, tied up with no shade and no water or anything. They were laying there, sleeping in the hot, Texas sun, baking to death. Ralph couldn't stop thinking about these poor dogs as he passed by and headed home. He couldn't stand it, so he turned around and went back. He walked up to the house and found no one was home. He then found a pan and a water hydrant by the house. He filled the pan and walked out to the side yard to deliver the refreshment. The dogs were still baking in the sun, asleep or maybe dead.

Ralph said, "When I got within about ten feet of the dogs, they jumped up and started barking and growling! Then they came at me! But they weren't tied up. They were loose! They chased me back to my pickup and almost got me before I jumped back into my pickup and took off!"

LOCK & LOAD—-WALMART PARKING LOT

My buddy, Dennis is always on time or early for any event. So, when he was an hour late for showing up at my house, I got worried. We were supposed to be leaving at 6 a.m. to go to Arkansas to scout out a place to go bear hunting. I didn't want to call him, because he is easily agitated and his disposition can be that of a bear that was just aroused from hibernation.

He finally called and said that he was on his way. He had been delayed. When he arrived, I asked if everything was OK.

"Here's what happened," he said. "I stopped at Walmart in Lindale to get a head lamp bulb. I was getting ready to replace the bulb. I had my hood up and had taken some things apart to get to the head lamp. I'd parked as close as possible to the front door of the store. It was 5 a.m. and an old Dodge pickup pulls in with a bunch of cane poles sticking out of the bed and about six, black guys inside the truck were drinking beer. They go in and come back out with their purchase and their truck wouldn't crank. One of the guys came up to me and asked if I could give them a boost. I told them "NO!"

One of them said, "We just need a boost. Our battery is dead."

"NO, I don't give anyone a boost, it's not good for my battery," I told them. "As I worked on my headlight situation, they pushed their truck closer to mine and hooked some jumper cables on my truck's battery. I walked around to the driver's door, reached in and grabbed a pistol, and jacked a round into the chamber as I came around to the front of the truck. I pointed it at them and told them to take the f__king jumper cables off of my truck. There were six of them and one of me and even though I had a gun they were being defiant and jawing at me."

One said, "Oh! I guess you don't like black folks!"

I told him, "No! I hate sorry sons-of-bitches like y'all! About that time, I thought I was going to have to shoot one, when I hear a gun cock behind me and to my left a little. Then I heard an old man say, 'I'm gonna' splatter this big fat one all over this parking lot, son. You take care of the other ones!' All of the jawing of the agitators had gone silent. I looked to my left to see an old man in overalls holding a single shot, 12 gauge, hammer-cocked and pointed at the biggest one of the six agitators."

"By this time, there was a crowd gathered at the front doors of Walmart, watching the stand-off. Within a few minutes, Lindale police department arrives—-one car with one skinny young cop who had his gun drawn. He approached cautiously and like a young Barney Fife ordered, 'Put down your weapons'. I laid my weapon down and raised my hands. The agitators raised their hands after they chunked their beers. The old man with the shotgun (we'll call him, Mr. Smith) remained defiant and stayed drawn down on the agitators."

"Hell, no! I'm not putting my gun down, Junior," Mr. Smith said.

"Please, Mr. Smith, put your gun down," Barney begged.

"Hell, no, Junior!" Mr. Smith said. "We used to not have these problems here in Lindale—-drunks running around at five in the morning, bothering people. Y'all are doing a sorry ass job of protecting people, Junior!"

"I'm sorry, Mr. Smith. We'll try to do better," Barney told him.

Evidently, Mr. Smith had known Barney all his life, because Mr. Smith was continually chewing on Barney's ass about the department's lack of keeping law and order. Barney gave up on getting Mr. Smith to surrender his weapon and began to ask question everyone else. Mr. Smith kept a bead on the agitators and railed on Barney about his shortcomings in law enforcement. In between questions, Barney would say. "Yes, Sir" and "I'm sorry, Sir" to Mr. Smith who was evidently well-known and respected in the community.

"Is your pistol loaded?" Barney asked Dennis.

Yes, It's loaded," Dennis replied and then told the officer what had happened.

The officer was questioning the agitators and getting their side of the story when backup arrived. All of the backup officers greeted Mr. Smith in a polite manner and did not request that he surrender his weapon. Mr. Smith gave each officer a good tongue lashing about the lack of law and order in town. Each officer replied with, "Yes, Sir. Sorry, Sir."

The agitators were arrested for public intoxication and their truck was towed. Dennis was let go after answering more questions, and Mr. Smith was still chewing on all the officers asses when Dennis drove away.

Remember Folks, it's better to have it and not need it, than to need it and not have it.

All you need is Jesus and a .45.

BLACK POWDER BUBBA

My buddy, Bubba decided to take up black powder shooting, so he had a rifle custom made. Bubba is well-versed in hunting and guns, but this was a bit of a new adventure for him. Bubba waited months before his custom-made, black powder rifle was finished and ready to pick up. He test-fired it at the gunsmith's shop and Bubba was dead on, driving nails with every shot. Bubba picked up some supplies and headed to his property down on the Sabine River to do some more shooting with his new prized possession. Bubba had bought a large container of black powder. He climbed into the bed of his pickup and opened up his supplies. He carefully and lovingly filled his rifle with powder, then projectile and wadding and put his percussion cap on the nipple. Standing in the bed of his pickup, he fired at a target.

Bubba in his haste to do some shooting had left his black powder container uncapped and when he fired, a spark from the rifle landed in the powder and BOOM! The explosion blew Bubba out of the back of his pickup along with everything else, tools, beer cans, black powder supplies, etc. Everything was blown out on the ground. There Bubba was——laying on the ground, sprawled out like a Walmart chicken. His hair was standing up and his face was black. He looked like a cartoon character who had been blown up.

Bubba sat up amongst the debris, smoke and soot still resonating from his body. He gathered his tools, beer cans and gun and went home. He survived and restocked.

UNOBTAINIUM

DEFINITION – A METALLIC SUBSTANCE YOU CANNOT POSSESS
Brother Cracker has a sneaky, smooth, subtle way with words. Sometimes, you have to watch him. In our M/C life, there was a young Brother we called Wee Man. Wee Man traded his softail deuce in for a new street glide Harley. Unhappy riding stock, this Brother ordered him some sure 'nuff, high dollar, expensive pipes that he had located on the internet. Pipes were ordered, payment was made. A month rocked on, but no pipes arrive. Two months rock on…still no pipes. About three months into the waiting period, and Wee Man was complaining about not having those super duper, cool, expensive pipes. He was still not sure when they would be shipped.

We all listened to his complaints and sympathized with him, except for Cracker. Cracker, being older and wiser, explained to Wee Man what the problem was. "You've evidently ordered some pipes made from unobtainium. That's why you can't get them," Cracker told him with a straight face.

"Unobtainium?" Wee Man asked.

"Yes, that's got to be the problem," Cracker affirmed.

"Is that unobtainium hard to get?" Wee Man asked.

"Most definitely—-it's impossible to get," Cracker said.

"If I would have known this, I wouldn't have ordered them," Wee Man replied.

By this time Cracker and the rest of us are laughing, while Wee Man is looking around at us trying to figure out what's so humorous. An explanation ensued, and Wee Man just shook his head in disgust.

"I should have known it was some bullshit like that!" Wee Man said.

(See definition in title.)

CRACKER QUOTES

"I can't believe you uncultured bastards don't like my Pickle Beer!"

CRACKER & THE LAW

Brother Cracker turned onto Highway 31 and set his cruise control on seventy miles per hour which was the speed limit. He noticed a Highway Patrol cruiser had made the turn at the same time he did and was right on the bumper of his Dodge pickup. After a few miles of the Highway Patrol being a foot off his rear bumper, Cracker thought, *"Wow, this guy's in a hurry, I guess!"* He eased over onto the shoulder in order to let him pass. The Highway Patrol takes the shoulder of the highway directly behind Cracker. Now, Cracker is wondering, *"What the hell?!"* He stops slowly, throws the truck in neutral and rolls down his window. He hears the officer on his public address system bark, "Driver, turn off the vehicle and put your hands out the window."

Cracker does as he was requested. The officer exits his cruiser and draws his service weapon while hiding behind his open door.

"Back toward the sound of my voice with your hands on your head," the officer orders. Cracker complies.

Upon reaching the officer, Cracker feels the cop's service revolver jabbed into the middle of his shoulders The cop shoves him against the tailgate.

"Are you in the habit of *NOT* pulling over when an officer is behind you with their lights on?" he asked.

"You didn't have your lights on," Cracker replied.

The cop pauses and looks over his shoulder at his cruiser which *doesn't* have any lights on. He doesn't seem to like this and begins to aggressively question Cracker about the amount of alcohol that he has consumed.

"I haven't had anything to drink today," Cracker said.

The cop asks him over and over again about how much Cracker has had to drink. The answer was always in the negative, "none". The cop did not like this answer and is already looking foolish for not having his lights on. He decided to search the truck. Cracker waits patiently, knowing there is nothing to find. After several minutes, the cop comes out of the trunk, holding a flask and grinning from ear to ear.

"Ah ha!" he says as he opens the flask and tilts it over until three or four drops come out and that's all. "Evidence!" the cop shouts.

"What evidence? You just poured it out on the ground!" Cracker said.

The cop stomps back to his cruiser and gets on the radio, checking driver's license, tags and anything else he can think of. After an extended stay on the side of the road and a lot of abuse of power, the patrolman states that he had just gotten his car out of the shop with light problems and that Cracker was free to go.

GO FIGURE...

OILFIELD HANDS

I have a friend, we'll call him Randy. He worked oil field jobs all his life, a hard-working good ole' boy. Randy would cuss every other word. He didn't mean anything by it; it's just the way he talked. It was part of the environment in this type of work as well as what I do. Randy's favorite cuss word was the F-bomb.

He could be talking about new tailpipes on his hot rod, "Those were some loud F-bomb pipes!" he would say.

"It's been a long, f-bombing weekend and I'm tired."

"I'm f-bombing hungry!"

"I'm so f-bombing happy!"

He used this word to describe everything as well as some other chosen words that are not publicly acceptable.

One day he came by the shop and was complaining that he had to take sensitivity training. He's an "old school" oil field hand and this new generation makes no sense to him.

"Sensitivity training?!" I asked. "Why? Why do you have to take sensitivity training?" I needed clarification on this since oil field hands are not known to be sensitive or are they concerned about other hands sensitivity that they work with.

"Yeah! The two, young (mother f-bombs) I was working with said I was cussing them!" he replied.

"Well, were you?" I asked.

"Well f-bomb, yeah! I was! Those little, mother f-bombers were sitting on their asses, not doing anything! I told them to get their f-bombing asses up and grab a chain and some tools and get busy! This is f-bombing oil field, you f-bombers, not daycare! Then they filed a complaint saying I was cussing at them! F-bomb them!

Well, Folks… I'm on Randy's side!

When Randy first found out where I lived (Highway 14, North of Hawkins) he said, "You know that black top road in front of your house?"

"Yes," I replied

"Well, there's some crazy mother f-bombers that live down that road. One is a real good welder and his kinfolk are good people, but they are some crazy, mother f-bombers," he explained. " I went down there one day, and they had a big set of oxygen and acetylene bottles. They took the oxygen bottle and strapped it to a go-cart with no engine on it. They were arguing about who was going to drive it while someone knocked the valve off the oxygen bottle. They finally put the go-cart in the middle of the black top road and shot the top off the bottle with a 30-06 rifle. The go-cart took off like a drag car and then after about one hundred feet it went airborne, like it had a booster rocket on it, getting higher and higher until the last time we saw it, it was flying over the top of some big, pine trees. Good thing nobody was driving! They're some crazy, mother f-bombers!" he said.

"Yeah! I know them. That's my wife's Father and his family, Donald Tate and Snort," I told him with a smile.

"Well, they're some crazy, mother f-bombers!" he said.

THE SPIRITS OF THE SABINE RIVER BOTTOM

I have a Masonic Brother whom I love as much as if he were blood kin. Kendell Land has been a part of my life for a long time and inspired me to follow my Masonic path as well as schooled me on guns and various other interests. He relayed a story to me about when he was a young man hunting in the Sabine River Bottom.

Kendell hunted everything in the river bottom such as ducks, squirrels, and deer. There were also still quail in East Texas in those days. Whenever he would get ready to go hunting, he would go by the store and buy a can of roast beef. It comes in the same kind of can as tuna fish, except it only comes in the large cans. Kendell would make his way into the river bottom and before he would start hunting, he would punch two holes in the roast beef can with a church key, one hole on each side like you do to a can of milk (if you don't know what I'm talking about, then you need to learn). Then he would place it on a certain stump in the woods, at his favorite hunting spot. By the end of the day or at least by the next morning, the can would be either gone or emptied of its contents and back on the stump without the label. The can was always returned empty and no label. If you ever try this, you will wonder how those big chunks of beef get extracted from the small holes. It was always bone dry inside the can. He never tried to see what got the can. He just placed the offering on the stump and then enjoyed good hunting in this area of the river bottom. He said it worked every time.

His Dad asked him what he was doing with the canned roast beef. After Kendell explained, his Dad shook his head and said, " Oh, ok! So, you're making offerings to the spirits of the river bottom, I guess." And then shook his head.

I tried this in the mountains of Oklahoma. The same thing happened to me, The label is always missing, and the can is always empty. Sometimes, the can does not come back. Yes, other critters may have carried it off. But, once it was returned empty with no label, and it had been smashed by a rock.

You know what I'm thinking—-Right?

If you hunt the Sabine River Bottom, you might want to give an offering to whatever is there, whether it's flesh and blood or spirit or a little bit of both.

You never know what's watching you!

LIKE A GOOD NEIGHBOR—-BUBBA IS THERE!

My buddy, Bubba, as I have aforementioned, is a great guy, a little high strung sometimes, but a great guy.

Bubba is a great neighbor who will do anything for anybody, anytime you ask. I should also mention that Bubba has eighteen wheelers, race cars, four wheelers, boats and lots of friends in and out of his shop and his house.

The house directly across the street from his shop was for sale, and I'm sure the realtor was showing the house mainly during the times that Bubba was gone and not there working on trucks or revving race car engines. One Saturday, several of us were gathered at Bubba's shop, it's kinda' of a gathering place for rednecks, truck drivers, drag car enthusiast and just good ole' boys like myself. Bubba's brother, Robert, was parked longways in front of Bubba's shop with his boat in tow.

Bubba, two or three of his brothers, myself and a couple of other guys were all standing around one side of the boat, eating crawdads, and we might have been drinking a beer, I don't remember, (the probability is pretty high). The truck and boat were between us and the house for sale. We were laughing, talking and eating those spicy crawdads when the realtor shows up with two prospective buyers. The realtor gets out of her car, Bubba waves at her and she waves back, then hurries the "victims"—-I mean the buyers into the house before they can meet any of the locals. Bubba is talking about the house for sale and how it's been on the market for a while and how he didn't understand why it hasn't sold yet. About forty-five minutes later, the realtor and buyers come out the front door and appear to be heading our direction, maybe they want to meet their new neighbors (this we will never know).

With the boat still between us and the approaching realtor and buyers, Bubba's brother, Robert, is propped against the boat with Bubba's boxer bulldog sitting at his feet. I'm facing the approaching trio and Bubba is beside me, slurping on spicy crawdads and swigging beer.

We're talking about how extra spicy these mudbugs are, when Bubba starts laughing and giggling, "I rubbed one of these spicy crawdads on his butt last week and he started running in circles and scooting his butt on the ground!" Bubba said as he pointed toward Robert (as it appeared). Bubba was actually pointing at the bulldog sitting by Robert, but from the approaching trio's view, it appeared as though he was pointing at Robert when he said this. Upon that statement, they did an immediate halt and about face with military-like precision and double-timed it back to the realtor's car, slammed the doors and spun tires as they fled.

We were all laughing at Bubba's story about the dog, when Bubba says, "I wonder what got into them? They *were* headed this way. I wanted to talk with them."

I recognized the problem when it happened and was laughing more about that than Bubba's story. I regained my composure and explained that from the visitor's perspective they couldn't see the bulldog, and it appeared as though Bubba was saying he rubbed a spicy crawdad on Robert's butt. We all erupted in laughter again!

Bubba said, "Damn! They're gonna think I'm crazy!"

We all just looked at each other and started laughing again. What an understatement, Bubba! We never saw those folks again, and it took a little time for the house to sell. I'm sure it's a challenge to sell a house next door to Bubba—-especially when he's home.

QUOTES FROM JASON (WILDMAN) KELLEY

"Never play cards with a nan named, Ace."
"Never date a woman with a tattoo of a dagger."
I'm part Irish and part German-I have no choice but to drink"

CROWD CONTROL – JASON (WILDMAN) KELLEY

In the early 1990's, the KKK had a rally in Tyler, and they had some opposition show up to protest the rally. Jason, being a curious individual, decided to go down and take a first-hand look at the situation. After several minutes of both sides yelling at each other and making demands, Jason steps up between the two groups and says, "Why don't y'all stop talking and get it on!"

Immediately, a mounted deputy gallops up to Jason and knocks him backwards with his horse.

"You had better shut up or else I'm taking you to jail for inciting a riot!" the officer said.

Jason regained his stance and replied, "Well, I'm tired of all the jawing that both sides are doing. They need to 'get it on' and see who the winner is!"

"I told you, shut up or go to jail!" the officer yelled and then rode away to keep the rest of the crowd under control.

Channel Seven News reporter was on the scene and upon seeing this occurrence, proceeded to interview Mr. Kelley, wanting to know his insights on the current situation. Well, after thirty or forty-five minutes of non-standard insights from Mr. Kelley, the camera's battery died and the interview ended. It was never aired.

GO FIGURE!!!

TEXAS BOUNTY HUNTERS

Now, Folks, I'm not politically correct. So, I'm going to forewarn you on this story. If it offends you, I'm sorry.

Back in the year 2000, there was a prison break here in Texas and seven dangerous inmates escaped and were on the loose for over a month. My friend, I'll just call him "Tex" (not his real name, not even his nickname) was doing a little bounty huntin' after he found out what kind of reward money was involved in the process. Now, Ole' Tex has done a little bit of everything from police work, military service, State of Texas, construction worker, teacher, coach, farmer, rancher and rodeo cowboy. He also went to Iraq as a private contractor and assists non-paying philanthropies such as Free Masons, Gideons (who distribute Bibles) to building churches in New Orleans after Hurricane Katrina hit.

Tex always wears a big cowboy hat, tall boots with his jeans tucked in and a big handlebar mustache. His Texas accent is unmistakeable. He's a little over six feet tall.

At this time, I talked to Tex at least twice a week, then for over a month I didn't hear from him. This was before everyone had cell phones. I went by his farm and saw that everything looked OK. The dogs had food and water, the horses were in the pasture and the house was locked. But there was no sign of Tex.

Then one Saturday, Tex pops in at Red's Barber Shop, he busts through the door with a big smile and grinning from ear-to-ear, he says "How the hell have y'all been?"

"Where the hell have you been? We've been worried about your crazy ass!" Red said.

"Well boys, y'all ain't gonna believe this shit!" Tex said.

"I been bounty huntin' for those escaped convicts!"

"They caught them weeks ago!" I told him.

"Yeah, I know. I was about three days behind them, getting closer by the day, and then I got a little side tracked and bought a thousand acres in Minnesota," Tex said.

"How the hell do you go from bounty huntin' three days behind the criminals to buying a thousand acres in Minnesota?" Red asked.

"Well, ya know, I was driving that little Ford station wagon and had my 25-06 rifle, because the reward was dead or alive, and I really figured dead was a lot less trouble. They went to Colorado, but I thought they were headed to the Canadian border through Minnesota. I went into a bar in some little town in Minnesota and ordered a beer. Everyone was staring at me, guess I kinda' stand out in Minnesota, I don't know. Well, anyways, one of the guys in the bar comes over and asks where I'm from. I say, "Texas."

He says, "Well, hell! We figured that! What are you doing here?" he asked me.

I tell him that I'm a retired police officer from Dallas, Texas, and I shot a Negro that was trying to rob me when I stopped at a gas station and I strapped him to the roof of my station wagon. At this point, they all run over to the window and looked at my car!

"When I got to your little town, I pulled into a gas station, and when the station attendant came running outside and took a look at my car."

"He said, "My God! What's that on the roof of your car?!"

I didn't even reply to him. I just fell to my knees and said, "Praise God! I'm home!"

"When I told the boys this, the whole place busted up with laughter and they started buying me drinks, and I told some more bullshit stories. One thing led to another, and they took me ice fishing and dog sledding. After several days of this along with drinking, I wound up buying a thousand acres from one of the relatives. It's on the Canadian Border, and I'm not sure if I bought some land in Canada or not!"

Tex is very personable and should have been a politician. He can talk his way into or out of anything…except nine years in a Louisiana prison…but that's another story!

THE BLIND MAN OF ROSE WOOD

One dark, winter night, I was heading West out of Gilmer toward Rose Wood. About three or four miles out of town, I could see a man walking toward oncoming traffic. He was on the side of the road by the ditch with a long stick tapping along the pavement. This led me to believe that he was blind. I had just crossed over a small, narrow bridge about a hundred yards before I got to him. I turned around and went back to see if he needed help. There wasn't much traffic on this country road at night, but he could fall in the creek or get run over. I pulled up beside him and rolled down my window. He stopped and kept facing forward holding his stick.

"Do you need a ride?" I asked.

"No," he said.

"It's awful dark on this road. You might get run over," I said.

"How the hell was I supposed to know it's dark. I'm blind," he replied in a pissed off tone.

"Well, there's a bad creek coming up in about one hundred yards. Don't fall in," I cautioned him.

"OK, thanks. I'll swap sides of the road," he said.

"There's a bridge up ahead and the creek's on both sides of the road." I said.

"Just leave me the hell alone and mind your own business," he said. The he took off again, heading toward Gilmer.

"You sure you don't want a ride?" I asked again.

"Hell, NO! I know how to get to Gilmer!" he shouted.

I got home and called Upshur County. Here's how that went:

"Hello, Upshur County Sheriff's Department," a male voice answered.

"Yes, there's a blind man walking down Highway 154 West. I think someone should know. You might want to check on him," I said.

"Oh, well. That's John Jones *(not his real name)*," he replied.

"I tried to give him a ride, but he refused. He seemed agitated and maybe confused," I said.

"Which way was he headed?" he asked.

"Toward Gilmer," I said.

"Toward Gilmer? Well, crap! I guess he's coming into town to cause trouble. He does it all the time. Comes to town and starts fighting, always fighting. Usually with people who want to help him. He's tough too, wins a lot of fights. People really don't want to hit a blind man, I guess," he said.

"Ok, whatever, I was just trying to help," I said.

"Thanks for the 'heads up'. I'll send some deputies to head him off and pick him up before he gets to town. I hope he doesn't resist and start fighting. He was mean before he went blind. Now, he's worse," he said.

I saw him once more after this time, but I did not offer my assistance.

THE "PIG OUT" PALACE

It was late June, and a few of my Brothers and me decided to make a run to Sparks, Oklahoma for a few days of Oklahoma Bike Week. We went from Texas to the Indian Nation Turnpike and exited off toward Oklahoma City. We stopped in Henryetta to grab some grub at a place called "The Pig Out Palace". With a name like that it's got to be good.

We rolled in on our bikes and parked. This was a previous life, but some of my current Brothers were there. We've been together a long time. It was me (Hillbilly), Cracker, Big Daddy, Bozo, Low Rider, ZZ, Trouble Too—I may have missed some but there's the gist of it.

A little gal seated us at a big table and handed out menus. She looked to be seventeen or eighteen years old and weighed maybe about a hundred pounds. She had a sweet personality, dark hair, tan skin and I'm guessing part Indian of some sort since we are in Oklahoma.

She must be a dedicated employee because she had the company logo tattooed on her arm—-yep, right on the outside of her upper arm there is a pig's head! On both sides of the head is a knife and fork and it reads "Pig Out Palace". And yes! I did confirm that it was real.

ZZ for obvious reasons is called ZZ *(God rest his soul)* because he looked like he should be playing guitar for ZZ Top. ZZ had forgot his glasses, so his son, Trouble Too, was reading the menu to him as he stared straight ahead while listening. The young waitress bent over between Cracker, Big Daddy and me and asked in a whisper, "Is he blind?" We were a little amazed at the question since she had been looking out the front door at us when we rolled up on our bikes. "Yes he is!" Big Daddy quickly answered.

"Really? That's amazing!" she exclaimed. How does he ride that motorcycle?" she asked.

"He rides with his right foot down, rubbing the pavement. When he feels the dirt and grass or bumps a reflector, he knows to get back over to his right or left," I said. My Brothers agreed.

"Oh, my! That is amazing!" she said.

When everyone had decided what they were going to eat, the waitress started taking our orders starting with ZZ.

"Are you the elder of this group?" she asked ZZ.

ZZ was totally unaware of the conversation concerning his ability to see. ZZ popped his head around and stared at her with his piercing blue eyes and said, "Well, yes I am. Thank you for asking."

The meal and service were great. The little waitress seemed curious and intrigued by the leather clad bikers, she was enthusiastically waiting on.

I wasn't the Road Captain, but I was on this trip. I wanted to reaffirm my next exit, so I asked the little waitress, "How much further to Shawnee?"

"I'm not sure," she said. "Never been there."

"It's only like sixty miles West of here," I said. "It's on the way to Oklahoma City," I doubled down.

"Yeah, I've never been there. I've never been anywhere except right here in Henryetta," she said. Then she smiled and said, "But in a few months, I'm going to San Francisco to spend a month with my cousin!"

We all congratulated her and tried to be supportive of her enthusiasm about the trip. We all paid our bills, tipping her well and then headed for our bikes. While some of the Brothers had a smoke before heading out, I pointed out the obvious, "I guess y'all know that little waitress is in for a big culture shock when she gets to San Francisco? She hasn't been sixty miles in any direction from Henryetta, Oklahoma, and San Francisco, California is going to be her first experience with the outside world! Damn!"

I take for granted my freedom to roam sometimes, but I guarantee you that I don't waste it. There's a big world out there folks…go see it, even if it's just sixty miles down the road.

DO IT!!

BOZO - (TROY)

My Brother, Bozo has been riding motorcycles for a long time and is full of stories. One of my favorites is about when he was down in South Texas working for some farmers and ranchers.

"I couldn't make enough money to get by, but I couldn't make enough money to leave either. I lived in an adobe hut and ate a lot of peanut butter and smoked a lot of weed. Finally, I got tired of it. I tied down everything I owned onto my motorcycle and put little Troy on the back. At this time, Little Troy was about seven or eight years old. I fired up my bike and told Little Troy, "Tell 'em bye, Little Troy." Little Troy flipped the farmers the bird and we got the hell out of there," Bozo said.

We used to do a lot of tent camping at M/C runs as well as some of our own events. Early one morning there was a commotion in Troy's tent, and we heard him cussing, something about "this damn zipper".

After several minutes of tent shaking and cussing, a knife blade stabbed through the front of Troy's tent. Then he stuck his pecker out the slit and relieved himself. "When you gotta' go, you gotta' go!" Troy said.

One night, after a party at the Club House, Troy decided to spend the night and sleep on the couch. One of our Sisters, knowing that Troy has false teeth, went over to him and asked if she could get him a bowl or cup for him to put his teeth in. "Nope, they'll be just fine right there," Troy said as he dropped his teeth into his boots that were setting beside the couch. Then he rolled over and went to sleep. I never found out if he remembered where his teeth were before or *after* he put his boots on.

QUOTES
MORRIS HALLMAN

"My life is an emotional roller coaster. Farrah Fawcett died, and I was down. Then I hear that Michael Jackson died, and here I am on top of the world!"

GRAND THEFT AUTO MONKEY

Anyone who knows me, knows that I love anything monkey related. So, when my son Cord called me and said, "I know you love monkeys, so I had to call and tell you about this." I knew it was going to be good. My son works for one of the big, three auto dealers and received a repair order for a vehicle that read *"replace all interior destroyed by monkey"*. After rereading and puzzling over the wording, he examined the SUV. Sure enough the whole interior of the vehicle had been destroyed, chunks were bitten out of the seats, dash, headliner, steering wheel and any pliable surface that a monkey could get into its mouth.

"It looked like something literally went ape shit crazy!" he said. "It was a total disaster inside this new SUV. All of the interior of the SUV had to be replaced! I bet State Farm will never believe this shit!" he said in between catching his breath from laughing.

I was dying on the other end of the phone, laughing as I pictured this monkey going on a rampage inside this vehicle ripping and biting everything as he has a tantrum. But, then it gets better. It turns out that the monkey isn't even the guy's pet. The monkey belongs to his girlfriend, and the monkey doesn't like this dude! He and his girlfriend had an argument, and she throws the monkey in his SUV, locks the doors and tosses the keys into the woods. While he's looking for the keys, the monkey is getting mad and going crazy! When the dude finds the keys and unlocks the door, the monkey tries to attack him, So, he shuts the door, and the monkey continues to destroy the dude's new SUV because he's really pissed now that the dude, he doesn't like, has tried to catch him. The monkey is finally apprehended and removed from the vehicle but not before he causes over ten thousand dollars in damages!

I have a great imagination, and the visions in my head of this monkey vandalizing this SUV from the inside are unforgettable.

Every time I think about it, it makes me laugh. Try to explain that to your insurance agent.

TRUE STORY!

"All you need to survive in this life is Jesus and a .45!"
- Ronald (Hillbilly) Armstrong

SNAKE BIT – JASON (WILD MAN) KELLEY

I've always been told that one of the deadliest snakes in the world was a coral snake. I didn't even know we had any in East Texas until Jason was bit by one. Jason is like a real-life Forrest Gump. If you can think of it, it's probably happened to Jason.

Jason was camped out at Tyler State Park with his wife and two sons, enjoying the outdoors and roping coons with his trotline string—-oh…wait, that's a different story.

Jason and his boys run across a snake that they identify as a King Snake. It is a colorful and a vibrant red, yellow and black snake that is harmless to humans but beneficial in catching mice and such. Jason picks it up, and it bites him between the thumb and forefinger. He thinks nothing of it and puts the snake in a jar for his boys to keep for a little while so they could study nature.

A little while later, Jason is cooking on the grill and drinking more whiskey. His wife and boys come sliding to a stop in their vehicle, and start screaming that he has to go to the hospital, They took the snake to a Park Ranger, and he identified it as a coral snake which is very poisonous. Jason was feeling light-headed, but he attributed that to the whiskey, which he always had readily available and partook of daily. Screaming and crying, his wife and children convinced him to go to the hospital. Upon arriving at the hospital with Jason and the snake, it was determined that a series of anti-venom shots needed to be administered into his stomach. Jason was beginning to feel a little more woozy and then realized that this feeling could not be attributed to the whiskey.

Jason is a lean guy and in good shape despite his smoking and drinking. After the anti-venom was given, his whole body was swollen to three time its normal size and the whites of his eyes turned blood red! The doctors were not sure which one could kill him first, the snake bite or the anti-venom. They told him that if he lived, he could never be given any type of anti-venom again.

"You're dying! You're dying!" his wife was screaming and crying. "You're dying right before my eyes!" she screamed.

"Shut up, damn it! You're making me nervous! I want a Marlboro!" Jason told her.

"You can't smoke in the hospital, and you need to stay in bed and lay still," the nurse told him.

"Get me a wheelchair!" Jason demanded of his wife. " I want a Marlboro and a bag of Doritos!" he said. "If I'm going to die, I'm gonna have a cigarette and something to eat!" Jason told them.

His wife rolled Jason outside the hospital and gave him a cigarette and some chips. He was swollen up like a bullfrog, all red-eyed like a devil, eating his chips and smoking. His wife was sobbing, thinking he was gonna' die.

After five days in ICU and several rounds of painful shots of anti-venom in the stomach, Jason was released from the hospital. The snake which they brought with them to the hospital for identification was taken to Caldwell Zoo for their snake exhibit.

Upon being released from the hospital and discovering where the snake was located, Jason wanted to go to the zoo and visit the snake that had bit him.

They arrived at the zoo and told their story. The zoo keepers were familiar with the story and the snake. Jason was not allowed to visit the snake. It seems that after its arrival, it had become ill and was in quarantine away from the other snakes.

"What's wrong with it?" Jason asked.

"We're not sure. We just know that its sick and lethargic. We don't know what made it sick," they said.

I'm pretty sure that Jason had so much whiskey in his blood that the snake got alcohol poisoning for real. I've never heard of a snake biting a person and the snake got sick.

Go figure!

You can see this snake today. It's on exhibit at the Caldwell Zoo in the reptile house.

LOVE LIFE ADVICE From
JASON (WILDMAN) KELLEY

Jason has vast experience with women, various women. But (yes...there's the but again), I promise you that he is really the last person you should take advice from concerning women.

Jason has never been one to cull women. I've seen him with everything from very beautiful women to one that I mistook for E.T. in a tube top.

I'm telling you, folks, my hand will cramp up before I can finish the list of women and their descriptions who Jason has dated.

There was one very pretty one that was dressed like a Jeannie or a Genie, and he was dressed like Spider Man. He picked her up at a costume party. I won't go into those details.

Then there was one that had hair like a carrot top and walked with a limp.

Then there was about four or five he was writing to who were in prison. When released from prison, Jason would play host to them at his house for two or three days before taking them wherever they wanted to go.

"A woman who's been locked up for five years will love you up!" Jason said.

He had been known to bail some of them out of county jail for fifty or a hundred dollars, and then after two or three weeks, go back on their bail if they started talking about fleeing.

"That's cheap company for two or three weeks," he said. "Just make sure they're in there for white collar crimes, credit card fraud, shoplifting, etc. No assault or murder convictions," he instructed. "I don't want no full-time night woman," Jason would say.

"Love is but a dung heap, and I am just a cock who climbs atop it to crow!" he would say, repeating the line from the movie Rob Roy.

Despite his rough and rugged ways, many women have found themselves falling in love with him. He would have none of it.

Jason is a "freak magnet". On more than one occasion, a wrong number call has turned into a date. I believe this has happened three times. One turned into an ongoing relationship. One such wrong number call invited him over for supper after a short conversation. He went over, they ate and enjoyed each other's company (if you know what I mean). It turns out that this lady had at one time had a car accident and has short term memory loss.

So, Jason calls her up in about a week. This is how it went:

Memory Loss Girl: "Hello."

Jason: "Hello, this is Jason."

Memory Loss Girl: "Do I know you?"

Jason: "Yeah, don't you remember me? I came over, we ate, we had sex."

Memory Loss Girl: " Oh, ok, you want to come over again?"

Jason: "Sure, I'll be there in ten minutes!"

After he arrives, he introduces himself again. Then, she explains her situation and medical or mental condition. This is ok with Jason, no problem. This goes on for probably a couple of years. No shit, really. Just like the movie "Fifty First Dates". I can't make up this stuff. Every time he calls, he explains who he is, and they have a date.

Another girl he went out with was a lesbian. After going out with Jason, she left her girlfriend. Her girlfriend was not happy with Jason.

There are other women and girls that we won't mention or go into details about. I'm trying to keep this book R-rated.

As a young man, there were women old enough to be his Mother, and now that he's older there are women young enough to be his daughter, not to mention some kissing cousins in between wives as in marriages not literally in-between…figured I better clarify.

With all that being said, I believe you can understand why I say, when actually looking for love or a relationship, you should ask someone else besides Jason for advice.

But, (yes…"but") a young man we know was desperately looking for someone to share life with and have a family, we'll call him "Billy". Young Billy was always asking advice from everyone he knew and never listening or applying the good advice he got.

One day, Jason offered a suggestion, "I go to Walmart to look for women. Yep, even when I don't need anything, I push a buggy around, and when I see a woman that looks good, I check for a wedding ring and then I strike up a conversation. Sometimes, it works, sometimes, it don't," he said.

After hearing this, young Billy decides to try it out. Three days later, he comes by our shop and seems a bit distressed. "What's wrong, Billy?" I asked.

"Well, I did what Jason suggested. I went to Walmart to find a woman, and it worked," Billy said."

"Wow! After all these years, I'm glad you met someone!" I told him.

"Yeah, well there's a problem," Billy replied. "After we talked and hit it off, I asked her out for a date. She said, 'Yes'."

"Ok, what's the problem?" I asked.

"It turns out, that she just got out of prison!" Billy said. "I don't know what she was in for, and I'm scared to ask. I don't think she's what I'm looking for," Billy said.

"Well, it serves you right! You never listen to anybody, and when you decide to actually take advice, you take it from *JASON!*" I told him.

"I'm not going to meet her, and I may have to change my phone number," Billy said.

"You're going to stand her up and change your number? That's not very nice!" I said.

"I can't go through with it. I just can't. My Mother would never approve!" Billy said.

And so ended the "would be" perfect relationship that Billy was seeking.

On another such occasion, I was within earshot of our wash rack at Carl Owens Truck RV Collision Center, when I heard Jason giving advice to Ira our wash rack steam cleaner man. Jason was advising him on ways to lure women to his house, evidently Ira was not having any luck attracting women.

"Just lie to them, Ira. Tell them you have a swimming pool. When they get there have a little kiddie pool, it's not a total lie," Jason advised.

"Sho-nuff?" Ira replied and then leaned closer to see what other advice Jason would offer.

"Yeah, do that and then tell 'em you've got all kinds of stuff to drink, even if all you have is one bottle of Ripple," Jason continued.

"Sho-nuff?" Ira exclaimed as he looked over the top of his horn rim glasses.

"Yeah, try it! It works every time!" Jason assured him.

By the time they get there and realize you don't have all this stuff, it's too late, and they're already there," Jason said.

"Sho-nuff? I'll try it!" Ira said.

Jason noticed me laughing and shaking my head. He came over with a big smile on his face.

"Did you hear what I was telling Ira?" he asked.

"Yeah, I heard. You're gonna get him killed, Them gals he talks to are gonna' show up to no pool, no booze, and then they're going to pull out a razor and cut his throat!" I said.

"You think so?" Jason said.

About a month later Ira didn't show up for work anymore. Not sure what happened to him. I haven't seen him since.

Be careful who you take love life advice from, folks. You might first want to know a little background about them.

QUOTES

"Saints burn grace like a 747 burns jet fuel."

——radio preacher, Tony Evans

BIG GREASY'S FUNERAL

As aforementioned, Jason Kelley is a "freak magnet". Jason had a fellow that he knew, pass away, (we'll call him "Big Greasy").

Big Greasy was not the best neighbor, citizen, father or husband. Jason took up residence in an area that he called, "Skitzerville". Jason didn't want to live there, but this was all that was available at the time. Big Greasy was a local resident, and I suppose you can guess what his occupation was living in Skitzerville. He was a full-time "Skitzer".

After one or two stays in the hospital and no intentions of changing his ways, Big Greasy expired.

Jason is always good to everyone. He has a big heart and will help anyone, even the crazy "Skitzers" that lived around him. If they needed gas, cigarettes, help working on vehicles or a ride, Jason was there to help. Big Greasy left a wife and four, small children behind.

They arranged his funeral and asked Jason if he would be a pall bearer. Jason agreed of course. When Jason arrived at the Church building where the funeral was taking place, he entered and asked one of the funeral directors where the pall bearers were supposed to sit.

"Have a seat wherever you want to. There's no casket to carry," the director said.

"What do you mean, there's no casket?" Jason asked. "They asked me to be a pall bearer," Jason said.

"Like I said, there's no casket, no body to carry. His wife and kids rolled the casket out to the cemetery themselves, grabbed some shovels, covered him up, and was back in here long before it was time for the funeral. They seemed to be in good spirits, and refused any help we offered," the director explained.

Jason said that the funeral went off without a hitch and without a body. After it was over, everyone offered condolences to the widow and children. They didn't seem to be put out about the situation. Maybe, they were glad to be shed of him and didn't want to take any chances. Only Jason could attend a funeral like this.

THE LETTER

My buddy, Jason Kelley, had fallen on hard times. Work had gotten slow, his vehicle broke down and the repair was expensive, along with a barrage of other financial demands. He decided that he needed to reorganize. So, after several days and hours of thought and wording, he penned a letter that was to be sent to all of the companies that he had a financial obligation to. The letter explained how he had suffered (a personal tragedy) and was unable to fulfill his financial obligation at this time, but he would like to work with them to satisfy this obligation at a later date if they were willing to work with him at this time. That is not the exact wording that he used in the letter except for (I have suffered a personal tragedy).

Now a personal tragedy can mean a lot of things to a lot of different people, for instance the death of a loved one, a natural disaster (i.e. tornado, flood hurricane, loss of a limb, diagnosed with a terminal or debilitating disease, etc.). He never misled anyone. It was the truth. He had suffered a personal tragedy————-he was short on money!

He asked me to read the letter and give my opinion about it. It was so well-written and convincing, that I was almost swayed to the conclusion that something horrific had happened to him, and I knew better! I liked it so much, that I made a copy of it in case I ever needed such a convincing letter.

What became known as "The Letter" was mailed out to all of Jason's bill collectors, prior to his ceasing to make payments. "The Letter" was well-received and the response was positive and appreciated by all who received it, usually resulting in a phone call to Jason that would go something like this:

"Mr. Kelley, we're so sorry to hear about your personal tragedy, and we will be glad to work with you in any way that we can. We hope that you overcome your personal tragedy, and look forward to resolving our financial agreement in the future."

A phone call, or a letter, or sometimes both were sent from Jason's bill collectors, sympathetic to his plight, except for one.

One lending institution demanded payment, regardless of his personal tragedy. They refused to work with him and threatened him with legal action.

Jason being the guy that he is, told them to proceed with legal action, and he would see them in court.

Court day came, and Jason represented himself. The court room was full of people and company lawyers who were suing one another for non-payment. It was Jason's turn, and the claimant gave documents and arguments for the reason of the lawsuit, and why the judge should find in their favor, causing Mr. Kelley to have a judgement against him and hopefully causing him to pay. One of the documents was "The Letter".

The Judge shuffled through the paperwork and had Mr. Kelley affirm that he had signed said documents, agreeing to pay as was laid out in the contract. Mr. Kelley answered in the affirmative, "yes, it was his signature" and "yes, he made the agreement to pay." The Judge shuffled a few more pages and came to "The Letter". He paused and read "The Letter". The Judge looked up after reading "The Letter" and addressed the company that was suing Jason.

"Have you read the letter that Mr. Kelley sent you?" the Judge asked.

"Yes, your Honor," the lawyer answered.

"It appears Mr. Kelley is trying to work with you and additionally has suffered a personal tragedy," the Judge pointed out. "It seems like you would try to work with the man instead of bringing him to court," the Judge continued.

By this time, everyone in the court room was paying attention. Evidently, this man had a good reason not to pay, and everyone wanted to know why the Judge's favor was leaning toward the defendant. The Judge read the short but well-written letter aloud to the court room and every defendant was taking notes.

"Your Honor, we still demand payment, and we have the legal right to receive payment or have a judgement against, Mr. Kelley," the stubborn lawyer said.

"Are you stating, you are not going to work with Mr. Kelley?" the Judge asked.

"No, Sir," the lawyer answered.

The Judge shook his head and looked at Jason. "Mr. Kelley, I'm sorry that you've suffered a personal tragedy, and I believe this company should try to work with you. But by law, I have to rule in their favor. I wish you the best, and hope that everything gets better for you. I'm very sorry that I have to make this decision, but by law, I have no choice. I would think that a company would be more willing to cooperate with you, considering what you've been through and that you've made an effort to work with them. I find in favor of the plaintiff," the Judge said.

Jason shuffled and collected his paperwork, turned and headed out the door. Halfway out of the building, the lawyer chased Jason down and said, "Mr. Kelley, let's make some kind of deal or arrangement to settle this."

Jason looked him in the eye and said, "I'll never pay you a dime. I tried to make an arrangement, but you decided to take me to court. I'll pay all the other companies I owe, but not you. You can go to Hell!"

Jason eventually paid everyone he owed, but not that company. To this day, he can threaten a bill collector with "The Letter", and they become very cooperative.

Never underestimate the power of a well-written letter or an Irishman!

MOTHER'S CAT

I'm thankful that the last eight years of my Mother's life were spent close to where I live, just about three hundred yards down the road from my home. I stopped by to check on her almost every day. Mother loved to laugh, and we did laugh a lot. We could find humor in things that other people could not. We would talk about family and friends, and retell funny stories, laughing as though it was the first time we had heard them, even when it was at least the hundredth time we had heard them! I miss her.

Mother never was a cat person, but my wife, Karen and I gave her a cat to help keep her company. Mother wasn't too keen on the idea at first, but she grew to love this orange-colored cat, just like it was family. She named the cat, Tigger. He was anti-social, but he loved Mother, and would come out of hiding when Karen or I were there, but the rest of the time, whenever company arrived, he would hide under her bed for the duration of the invader's visit.

Mother had a home health nurse that came by once a week and sometimes a physical therapy nurse who would come by once a week. Mother loved to talk to people. "The Gift of Gab", she had it. I'm pretty sure that my two daughters, Amanda and Leslee, have it also. Mother would talk to her nurses and tell them all kinds of true stories about her life and her different husbands. She also talked about her cat a lot and all the things that he would do and how he would act when he saw bird as he sat in the window sill, etc., etc.

One day, I told Mother in a joking manner, that the nurses were going to think she was crazy, talking about her cat, because he was always hidden, and you couldn't tell she had a cat, other than food and water bowls that were always full and a litter box that was always clean. Mother kept a spotless house.

"You know, I never thought about that. He always hides when they come by, and they've never actually seen him," she said.

I didn't think much more about this, but evidently she did. She didn't want the nurses thinking that she was a mental case, so she trapped Tigger in the bathroom and made the nurses go in and look at him.

"See, I really do have a cat. I'm not crazy," she told them. "My son said, that y'all thought I was making it all up about my cat and thought it was funny. I just want to make sure that you know, that I'm not crazy—-well, maybe I am a little crazy, but I do have a cat!" she said.

When I stopped by that evening, she told me what she had done. We had a big laugh, then I told her '"Well, I guess I'll call your nurse and tell her that you caught the neighbor's cat to show her, so you wouldn't think she's crazy!"

We had a big laugh about this, and she said, "You better not! I like to have never trapped him in the bathroom."

A few weeks later, they changed nurses, and her new nurse was a guy who weighed about four hundred pounds. Mother, not wanting to spend days trying to trap Tigger in the bathroom again for viewing purposes, decided to get one thing clear right away. She had the big guy lie down on the floor and look under her bed at Tigger.

"See, I have a cat. He hides under the bed when company comes. So, when I tell you I have a cat, I really do have a cat," she told him. "Yes, Ma'am, I understand," he said.

I stopped by and Mother told me about the new nurse and what she made him do. Mother told me she wasn't sure that he was going to be able to get up from the floor without some help, but he finally made it!

I said, "Mother, what if Tigger wasn't under the bed when he was looking, and he just agreed with you because he thought you were crazy. I bet he wrote in his report: 'Mrs. Beaird has an imaginary cat. She forced me to look under her bed to affirm that she had a cat. I agreed so as not to upset the patient'. We were both laughing until we cried, and our sides were hurting.

"Don't tell me that ! Now, I don't know if he really saw Tigger or not!" she said.

She continued to trap Tigger and show him to any new nurses she had. I believe this made him even more anti-social. We had many good laughs about that cat and various other things. Tigger lives with me and Karen now, and after many months of therapy from Karen, he has overcome his anti-social behavior.

I miss Mother's laugh, her smile, her sense of humor. She is missed and loved.

Born: Edna Virginia McEwin, My Mother

October 16, 1937, Chicota, Texas

Her friends called her Gina.

Her nine brothers and sisters sometime called her Junior because she was the youngest.

MY BROTHER—-WE HUNTED

After a lifetime of living in the country and in the mountains, my Brother, Dennis Renfro, got a job in the big city, and he sits and listens to guys talking about deer hunting. He just smiles and nods his head. They don't know that they're talking to one of the greatest deer slayers in Texas. They talk about filling feeders with corn and sitting in box stands and tree stands purchased at retail stores, expensive leases and hunting equipment. Ha, ha, ha. I can't help but laugh to myself when I hear the same discussions.

We hunted because we needed to and because we love it. We hunted. We hunted!

We looked for signs, rubs, tracks and trails. We sometimes only had a .22 rifle. We hunted on the ground and tracked deer up to where they stood. We climbed up into trees with good limbs for sitting. We nailed used boards with used nails to trees for makeshift stands. We hunted from ragged, rotten stands that were nothing but 2'x4's nailed to trees, deep in the woods, where they had been abandoned and long forgotten. We hunted in places where we had permission to hunt with no fees, and nothing expected in return, except maybe a hind quarter or back strap. We hunted in places, we weren't supposed to be, private property, game management land, army corp property, government property that covered eighty thousand acres at one time, wheat fields, alfalfa patches, gravel roads and highways,. We hunted in the heat, we hunted in the freezing cold, we hunted in the rain and snow. We hunted in the daytime, we hunted at night. We ate everything we killed, and we were not hunting trophies, not that some didn't come along every now and then.

Some people don't understand this—-and I don't expect them to do so. If you've never hunted because you need to—-then you never really hunted.

WE HUNTED!

QUOTABLE QUOTES
&
A FEW WORDS TO LIVE BY

"There are two things that I don't mess with, the U.S. Government and an Apache Squaw."

—-Sam Whiskey aka Burt Reynolds

I've been wedded, bedded, loved and let down. It hasn't always been fun, but at least it's been natural."

"Fortune favors the prepared."

—-unknown

"Whenever I'm asked about not wearing a jacket in cold weather, my reply is: 'I was cold once. It was minus fourteen degrees, we were deer and elk hunting in the Rockies, North of Pagosa Springs, Colorado. I had a Walmart sleeping bag. After that, everything seems warm.'
—-Ronald E. Armstrong

"Isn't life strange?!. By the time you're old enough to know what you want...
...you've had so much of what you didn't."
"To be able to be truly loved, you have to be willing to be rejected."
—-unknown

"Don't jump off a cliff, just for a brief sensation of flying."
—-Ronald E. Armstrong

"Desires of the heart, when unobtainable, are the most egregious."
—-unknown

"Men become men in the presence of other men"
—-unknown

"You never know about a woman or a cow until they've been on your range for a while."
—-Gil Favor, Trail Boss

"Reach the unreached and then teach the reached for Jesus."
—-Woody Woodard

"God's grace is His crazy love that even his Apostles struggled to understand."
—-Charles Stanley

"He cried like a baby, he screamed liker a panther in the middle of the night. Then he saddled his pony and went for a ride. It was the time of the preacher in the year of '01. Now the lesson was over, and the killing begun."
—-Willie Nelson

"I have childish curiosity sometimes. I would like to know things that I can't get answers to, only theories. Like whom and how did mankind learn to make metal? The Bible says that Tubal Cain was the first worker of metal. I believe this, but who taught him. How did he learn? From angels, sent by God of fallen angels sent by Satan?"

—-Ronald E. Armstrong

"Drinking and having sex were the biggest sins when I grew up. But there were people who didn't do either and did not have a relationship with Jesus."
(I forget who said this, but it stuck in my head.)

"When the old die, we lose wisdom, when the young die, we lose hope."
—-An American Indian

"Nobody listens!"

—-Ronald E. Armstrong

"All you need to survive in this life is Jesus and a .45"
—-Ronald E. Armstrong

"Any job is just as exciting as you want to make it."
—-Dennis Renfro (my Brother)

"Anything you love may be a lot of trouble."
—-Morris Hallman

"If God didn't want me shooting deer at night, He wouldn't have put reflectors in their eyes."
—-Charles Beaty aka The Prince of Poachers

"The above statement is straight out of the 903 area code."
—Marty Mabry

"Life is uncertain, but death is sure."

—Dean Campbell, truck driver

WOODY WOODARD
&
THE DRAFT – VIETNAM

My preacher, Woody is a great guy, committed to God and sometimes people may think that *HE* needs to be committed. LOL!

Seriously, Woody is sold out to Jesus, and you see it in his actions and hear it in his prayers when he prays for people. Woody is the preacher of Iron Horse Biker Church, and he look every bit the biker and sounds, every bit the preacher. He is seventy-six years old at the time of this writing. He rides his Harley several times a week, probably every day and not just short rides. His beard is long and gray as well as his hair with hints of black, and when he gets off his Harley, he puts on his Cowboy hat—-always. He sold out to Jesus when he was in his twenties after many years of drug addictions and hard living.

We could fill a book with the stories of his previous life, but he strongly resists any glory given to those days. He loves people, and believes his actions prove more for Christ than his words.

He's always trying to help folks. He gives and ministers to the homeless as well as everyone in our M/C community. I know he's real about how he feels and cares for people. I can feel it in his touch and hear it in his prayers. He looks rough and tough, but his kindness flows from him when he speaks and prays.

He always preaches, prays and counsels with a touch of humor. Often times, he unintentionally makes me laugh.

During one of his sermons, he reflected upon his previous life of drugs and prodigal living at which time he received his draft notice for Vietnam. He did not want to go, that was a solid fact. He reported to the enlistment office and had a wide array of reasons why they should not accept him. One of those reasons being (and this is just a lie that he invented)) he was gay!

As I sat and listened to this preacher, who looked more like Charleston Heston's Moses in the Ten Commandments Movie with a cowboy hat and dark glasses than he did a stereotypical preacher, it struck me funny, and I began to laugh uncontrollably, and then to top it off he says, "I told them I was gay, but unwilling to do anything to prove it."

He was drafted into the Army anyway. The first day in country, he was court marshaled for drug possession. Somehow, he beat the charges, and instead of being assigned to some clerical duties that he had been trained for, they required him to carry one of those big radio antennas on his back, and he had to jump in and out of helicopters with it on his back. He served his country and was honorably discharged. Thank you Woody for your service and all you do now.

FAKE TATTOOS & FELONS

I think we can all agree that as teenagers go, most are not too bright. They may be intelligent, but sometimes they don't have the life experience needed to make good decisions in some situations. Some are less bright than others. This is a story about two young men in Hawkins, Texas who came up with a really, really stupid idea. We will call them "Casey" and "Jeremiah". This may or may not be their real names.

So, let's start with the big news headline of the day on that day.

"WANTED! Felon on the loose in Hawkins, Texas. Armed and dangerous. FBI and local authorities have set-up a command station at the local VFD and a huge man hunt is underway around the Hawkins area which includes the vast property owned by Exxon which is wooded and has gravel and dirt roads winding around to oil and gas wells.

Jeremiah and Casey were excited that there is something like this happening in their small town which has one traffic light and a water tower. They listen to the news with enthusiasm, and then the news shows a picture of the felon and gives a description of his tattoos and what he is wearing. Jeremiah determines that Casey looks a little like the wanted felon and persuades him to wear a white, "wife beater" undershirt like the felon is wearing. And with a little more persuasion, he talks Casey into letting him draw tattoos on him which match those of the felon (y'all see where this is going, right?) BINGO! Jeremiah has created a look alike of the armed and dangerous felon who's wanted by the FBI! Both are very pleased with the transformation, and to top off this feat of stupidity, they head out to the area where the FBI are looking for the felon, "to assist them"!!

Yeah, folks, I can't make this stuff up and expect you to believe it!

After arriving in the search area, and wandering about on foot, up and down the Exxon roads and four-wheeler trails, they came face-to-face with an FBI agent! Startled, the agent pulls his gun and orders them to freeze! The agent, who thinks he has captured the felon and some unknown criminal that's assisting him, calls it in on his radio and reports the hunt is over!

Of course, Casey and Jeremiah are trying to explain, "You've got the wrong guy!"

"Yeah, right! Clothes match, tats match, I've got the right guy!" says the agent.

They were handcuffed and taken to the car, then transported to the command center which was at the VFD. Did I mention that Casey's Father was the Fire Chief? They bring the dangerous criminal into the VFD along with his co-conspirator.

I'm sure the look on Casey's dad's face was priceless. I'm certain that confusion was running rampant when he said, "That's not your felon, that's my son! Right, sure! His clothes match, tats match, kinda' looks like an open and shut case. But I promise you, he's not your felon!"

After much discussion, questions, and I'm certain some harsh words to Casey and Jeremiah they were released with the order "to wash off that well-drawn tattoo that helped convince the FBI that you're not that felon".

Good thing the agent wasn't a shoot first, ask questions later kind of guy. I'm sure the FBI and local authorities never expected anything like this, that's just plain stupid!

I'm telling you folks this is the dumbest thing that I've ever seen or heard of. Well, top ten anyway!